Nigel Short's Best Games

Batsford Chess Library

Nigel Short's Best Games

International Grandmaster Raymond Keene

An Owl Book
Henry Holt and Company
New York

Henry Holt and Company, Inc.
Publishers since 1866
115 West 18th Street
New York, New York 10011

Henry Holt® is a registered
trademark of Henry Holt and Company, Inc.

First published in the United States in 1993 by
Henry Holt and Company, Inc.
Originally published in Great Britain in 1993 by
B. T. Batsford Ltd.

Library of Congress Catalog Card Number: 93-79188

ISBN 0-8050-3051-4 (An Owl Book: pbk.)

First American Edition—1993

Printed in the United Kingdom
All first editions are printed on acid-free paper.∞

10 9 8 7 6 5 4 3 2 1

Advisor: R. D. Keene, GM, OBE
Technical Editor: Andrew Kinsman

Cover illustration by Brian Robins.

CONTENTS

Algebraic Notation

The moves contained in this book are given in what is known as 'Figurine Algebraic' notation. This describes a very simple and easy way of writing down the moves. Readers familiar with the system can jump ahead to the games themselves, but those who are comparatively new to the game or who have only learned the older 'English Descriptive' notation, will find what follows helpful. It is assumed that the reader already knows how to play chess.

Each piece is represented by a symbol called a 'Figurine', as follows:

	Symbol
Pawn	–
Knight	♞
Bishop	♝
Rook	♜
Queen	♛
King	♚

The squares on the chessboard are described by co-ordinates consisting of a letter followed by a number (see Diagram). For instance, the square marked with a cross is called 'e4'. This follows exactly the same principle as reading off a reference on an A–Z street guide or road map. Everybody can pick this up in a matter of minutes. There is no mystery to it all!

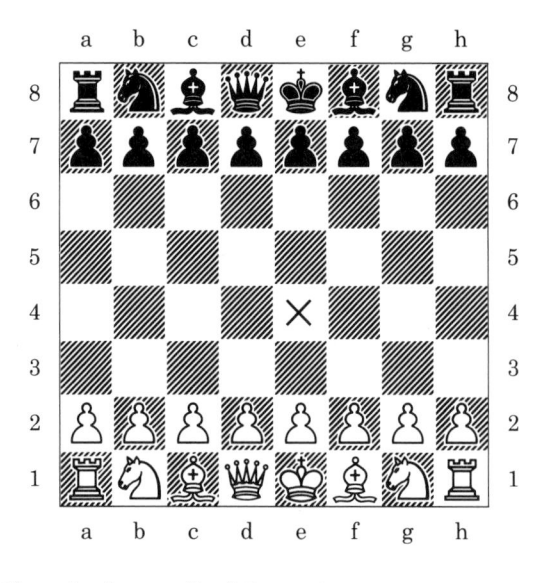

Symbols and abbreviations

+	Check
!	Strong move
!!	Brilliant move
?	Bad move
??	Blunder
!?	Interesting move

INTRODUCTION

A 12-year-old boy sits at a chessboard. Facing him is a formidable and deadly opponent. The man is an experienced master, a player who has beaten one World Champion and himself won the British Championship a record ten times. The scene is Brighton in the summer of 1977. The boy is Nigel Short, the first pre-teenager ever to compete in the British Championship, and the hardened veteran is Dr Jonathan Penrose.

After a few moves of play, to the amazement of the onlookers, Penrose offers the boy a draw. To the even greater consternation of those looking on, the boy declines the offer. The game proceeds. First, Penrose almost loses his queen, and then, faced with inevitable checkmate, on the 41st move, the shattered master concedes defeat.

That sensational game announced the arrival of a new chess prodigy, in the tradition of young geniuses of the calibre of Paul Morphy, José Capablanca and Bobby Fischer. Since his own auspicious debut, Nigel Short has progressed with meteoric brilliance. He has indisputably become the greatest British chessplayer in the history of the game. He has reached a world ranking of number three and has been the inspirational leader of the grandmaster-packed English team, spearheading them to three Olympic silver medals, behind only the hitherto dominant Russians.

The highlight of Nigel Short's career so far was his victorious challenge in April 1992, to the living chess legend, Anatoly Karpov, in the semi-final of the World Chess Championship qualifying competition. Karpov held the world title for ten years, until he was deposed by Gary Kasparov. He is one of the three or four greatest players chess has ever seen.

Beating Karpov raised Short to the pinnacle of world chess, a position he reinforced in January 1993 by his victory over the Dutchman Jan Timman in the final of the World Championship qualifying competition, a result which enabled Nigel to challenge Gary Kasparov in a match for the World Championship.

So, what has made Nigel so devastatingly effective over the chessboard? Short is a tough pragmatist, self-educated and self-reliant. His physical appearance belies his ruthlessly aggressive and starkly individualistic approach when in play. Short is tall and slender, hesitant, softly spoken and mild, not at all the stereotype of the mad genius which Bobby Fischer fitted so well.

Short's career has been studded with glittering successes, first prizes in tournaments and match victories around the world, but there have also been, as distinct from the careers of Kasparov and Karpov, the occasional equally stunning setbacks. When he was only 14, Short was thrown, by well-meaning chess officials who wanted to encourage and accelerate his progress, into the shark pool of the 1980 London international tournament, with a line-up including the world title challenger, Victor Korchnoi, who was not even able to win first prize, such was the strength of the competition. Short was unable to avoid a disastrous last place. He was just too young and inexperienced for this murderous field. However, Nigel has since overcome these problems, and when he went one down in the semi-final against Karpov, he did not become discouraged.

What was Nigel Short's grand strategy in the all-important match against Karpov? Both he and Karpov, as opposed to the brilliantly destructive Kasparov, are architectonic players, pure stylists who seek to expose and make visible the inner harmonic workings of the dynamic interplay of the pieces. Where others would simply see a discordant chaos of clashing chessmen, Short and Karpov perceive almost infinitely beautiful patterned networks. In the past, Short has laid the accent on such pure thought: the superiority of his thinking apparatus over that of his opponents. But defeating Karpov required a new dimension of combat. Physical as well as mental fitness now became of vital importance — it may even have proved to be the deciding factor.

For the showdown against Karpov, the 26-year-old Short was determined to be at the peak of physical strength. The plan was to play longer games and wear down his 41-year-old (and slightly paunchy) opponent. The war of attrition, to drain Karpov's energy, would suddenly transform into a blitzkrieg when the former champion was suitably enervated. This did, indeed, happen. Games three, four and five of this ten-game match were mind-exhausting marathons, but then Short struck to take games six and eight with lightning victories. Chess may seem all in the mind, but the mind is connected to the body.

The challenge to Karpov took place in the Andalusian city of Linares in southern Spain. Linares is famous for two other things apart from chess. It was the birthplace of Himilce, the wife of Hannibal, and the city also boasts a fountain from which Hannibal is reputed to have drunk. Local legend has it that those who, emulating the Carthaginian general, drink from this fountain, will inevitably return.

Having stormed the international chess heights, Short is on the threshold of becoming one of Britain's select millionaires to have derived their fortunes solely from prowess at sport. He will be the only one to have climbed so far on the ladder of financial reward through success in a sport where the primary battlefield is the mind.

How much money could Short potentially earn from chess? The prize purse escalates off the Richter scale as the World Championship cycle progresses. The pot of gold at the end of the chess rainbow beckoning Short is a staggering £1.7 million. This is a prize fund, divided solely between Champion and Challenger, on offer for the World Championship match against Gary Kasparov himself.

Some critics complain that, even though Short has pulled it off against Karpov and Timman, he will stand no chance against Gary Kasparov, the Russian who has monopolised the title since 1985. For a ten-year period from 1981 to 1991, Kasparov never fared worse than a share of first prize in every important tournament in which he entered. This is a colossal record in any sporting discipline, let alone chess, where one tiny error in the thousands of moves played in a tournament can mean the difference between first prize and top of the also-rans. Kasparov has seemed invulnerable and invincible.

Yet his nimbus of invincibility is increasingly being dispelled by disrespectful rivals. At a tournament in Dortmund, concurrent with Short's match against Karpov in Linares, Kasparov suffered the indignity of losing both to the brash teenager, Gata Kamsky (USA, formerly USSR) and the veteran German, Robert Hübner who, at the other end of the scale, is almost 20 years' Kasparov's senior.

Having passed the test of fire represented by overcoming Karpov and Timman, a challenge by Short against Kasparov could stand every chance of success. Nigel Short could become the first British World Chess Champion. He would thus revive, at a stroke, the glories of British chess of the mid-nineteenth century. Then, players such as Howard Staunton and Joseph Henry Blackburne kept Britain at the forefront of world chess and Simpson's-in-the-Strand, now a famous traditional restaurant, became a congregating point for every master and champion. With Nigel Short as World Champion, London would replace Moscow as the capital of world chess.

This book contains twelve of Nigel Short's best games, including victories over Boris Gelfand, Anatoly Karpov and Jan Timman on the way to his challenge for the world title.

GAME ONE

White: Nigel Short
Black: Dr Jonathan Penrose
British Championship, Brighton 1977
Sicilian Defence

There have been several notable prodigies throughout the history of chess; Paul Morphy, José Capablanca, Samuel Reshevsky, Bobby Fischer — all of whom shone by their 12th birthday. This game enabled Nigel Short to join that elite group.

Nigel's career up until now had already made him the youngest-ever qualifier for the British Championship. As discussed in the introduction, however, this game took the chess press and public by storm.

After this win the unthinkable seemed possible. A 12-year-old might actually win the British Championship. However, Nigel over-exerted himself during the middle weekend of the two-week long tournament, dashing up to London to challenge the World Champion Anatoly Karpov in a simultaneous display. Nigel lost to Karpov and returned to Brighton overtired so he did not perform as brilliantly in the second week. However, this game was memorable enough!

1	e4	c5
2	♘f3	e6
3	c3	

Rather a slow treatment, doubtless designed to avoid the master's superior knowledge of opening theory. The usual move is 3 d4.

3	...	♘f6
4	♗d3	

An unusual development of the bishop, in front of White's d-pawn, but not bad if White can get in ♗c2 and d4 in the near future.

4	...	b6
5	0-0	♗a6

A strange response. Why not 5 ... ♗b7, which would seem considerably more natural?

The young Nigel in action against former World Champion Vasily Smyslov (Camera Press).

| 6 | ♗xa6 | ♘xa6 |
| 7 | d4 (1) | |

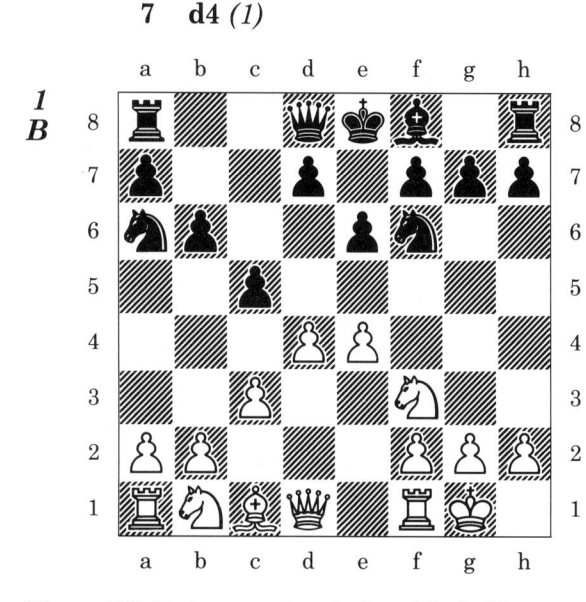

Thus, White's opening is justified. Short now controls the centre, the most important part of the chessboard.

| 7 | ... | cxd4 |
| 8 | ♘xd4 | ♗e7 |

The neat point is that 8 ... ♘xe4 fails to 9 ♕e2 ♘ac5 10 b4! or 9 ♕e2 ♘ec5 10 b4! In both cases, Black loses a knight.

| 9 | e5 | ♘d5 |
| 10 | ♕g4! | g6 |

A serious concession, but if 10 ... 0-0 11 ♗h6 wins the exchange (rook for bishop).

| 11 | ♗h6 (2) | |

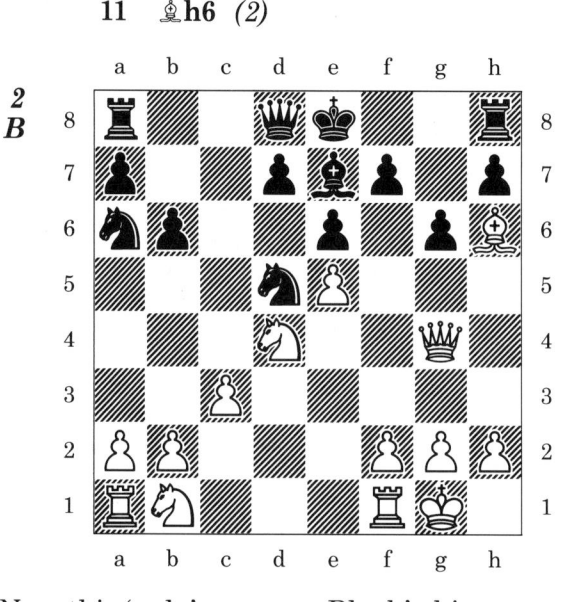

Now this 'only' maroons Black's king, but it is still sufficient to grant White a substantial advantage.

11	...	♘c5
12	c4	f5
13	♕f3	

Even stronger is 13 ♕h3 to be followed by 14 ♗g7. This would effect a decisive penetration of Black's king's flank.

13	...	♘c7
14	♘c3	♕c8
15	b4	♘b7
16	a3	♘d8
17	♘db5	♘xb5
18	♘xb5	

The knight strives for a dominating outpost on d6. Penrose's handling of the opening has manifestly been a disaster.

18	...	♘c6
19	♗g7	♖g8
20	♗f6	a6

21 ♗xe7 ♔xe7 *(3)*

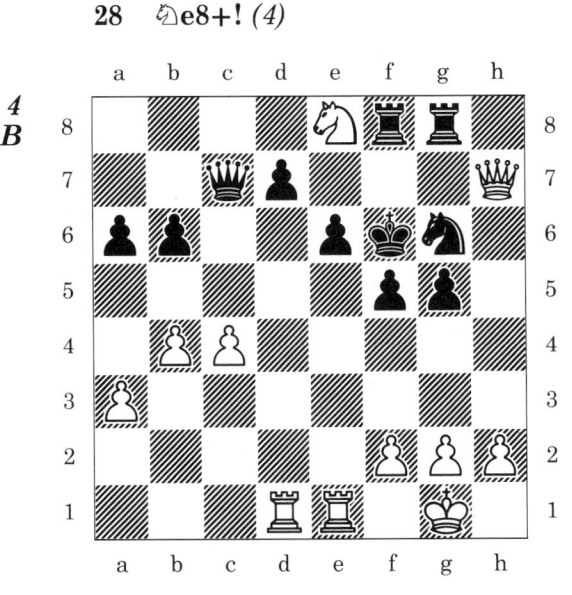

Black offered a draw here, but it is too late. Still, how many 12-year-olds would have refused against a ten-times British Champion? Short's resolve here shows what poise and self-confidence he already possessed.

22 ♘d6 ♕c7
23 ♕g3 g5

Or 23 ... ♘xe5 24 ♖ad1 ♘f7, and not now 25 ♘xf5+ ♔d8 26 ♕h4+ g5 27 ♕xh7 ♖h8! but 25 ♕h4+, when 25 ... g5 26 ♕xh7 leaves Black tied in knots.

24 ♕h3 ♘xe5
25 ♖ad1 ♖af8
26 ♖fe1 ♘g6
27 ♕xh7+ ♔f6

28 ♘e8+! *(4)*

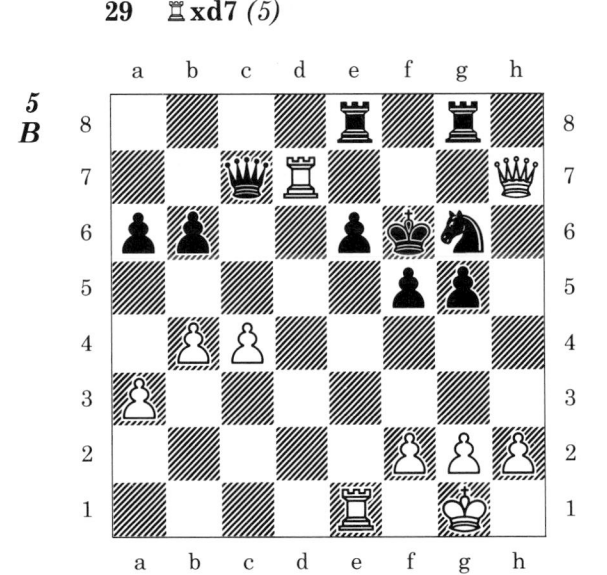

An incisive combination, gaining material. This is a quite brilliant tactic for such a young player.

28 ... ♖xe8
29 ♖xd7 *(5)*

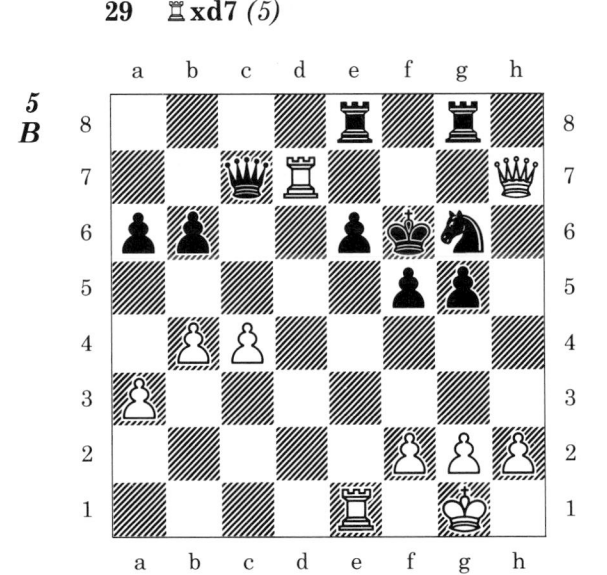

The threats of checkmate along the seventh rank force Black to surrender his queen or the exchange, i.e. rook for knight. Penrose prefers the latter, but it only postpones the day of execution.

29 ... ♖e7
30 ♖xc7 ♖xh7

13

31	♖xh7	♖c8
32	♖a7	♘e5
33	♖xa6	♘xc4 *(6)*

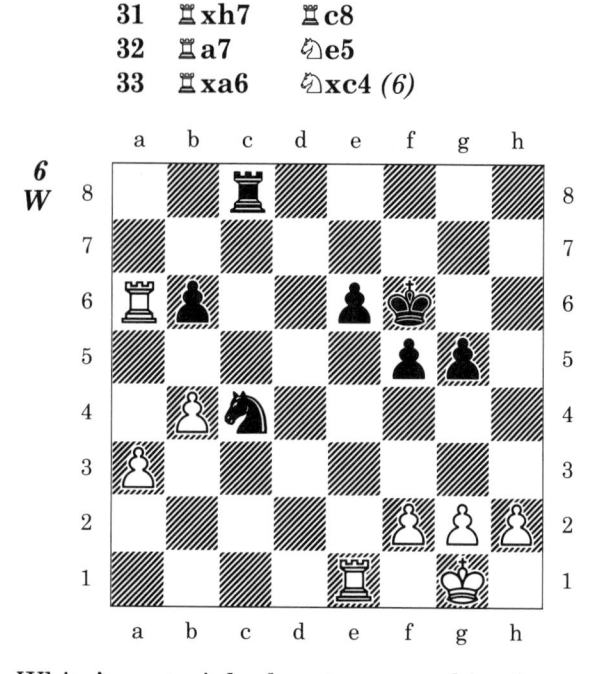

White's material advantage, combined with his more active pieces, mean that his victory cannot be postponed for much longer.

34	a4	♔e7
35	a5	♖b8
36	axb6	♘xb6
37	b5	♔d6
38	h3	♔d5
39	♖aa1	♘c4
40	♖ad1+	♔c5
41	♖xe6	**Black resigns**

That a 12-year-old should defeat the ten-times British Champion, and in such dashing style, created a national sensation at the time! A new chess genius was clearly announced by this game, the most dramatic of the 1977 British Championship. Perhaps Nigel Short was to be the British Bobby Fischer that we had all been awaiting for so long.

GAME TWO

White: Tony Miles
Black: Nigel Short
London 1982
King's Indian Attack

Between 1977 and 1982 Nigel continued to make rapid progress, tying for first prize in the 1979 British Championship and, the next year, earning the International Master title! But Nigel entered a real shark pool by playing in this super-strong London tournament, which featured twelve grandmasters including Karpov, Andersson, Timman, Miles, Spassky, Nunn and Speelman. Although Nigel finished in last place, a win against Tony Miles, England's Olympic number one at that time, must have been exceedingly gratifying.

1	g3	♘f6
2	♗g2	d5
3	♘f3	c6
4	0-0	♗f5

A good solid reply to White's restrained and subtle flank opening. Black sensibly sets up a bulwark of pawns in the centre.

5	d3	e6
6	♘bd2	h6

To provide a retreat for his queen's bishop against the possibility of ♘h4.

The first British Grandmaster, Tony Miles (Mark Huba).

Britain's first World Championship Challenger (Mark Huba).

7 ♕e1 (7)

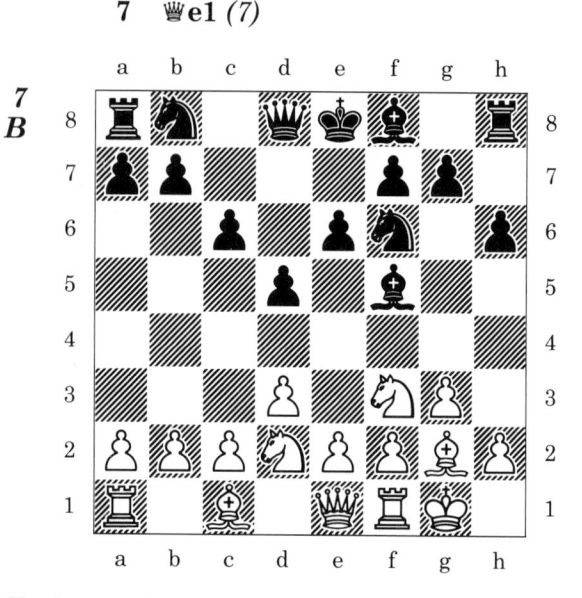

13 ♘e1   b5 (8)

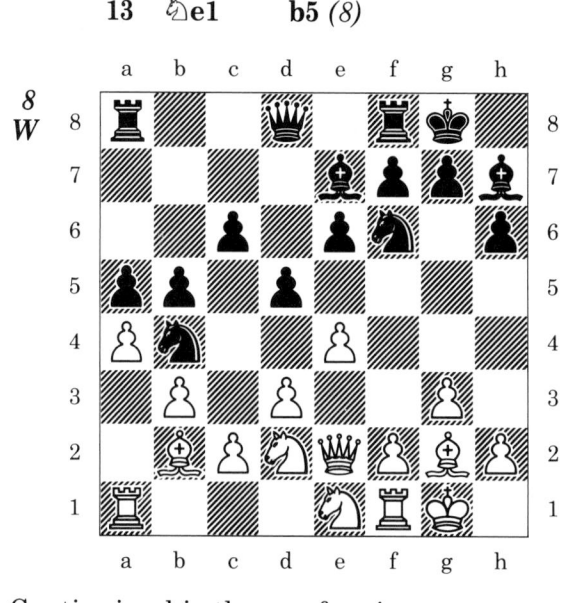

Trying to force through the central push, e4. White could, of course, also continue with 7 b3 plus ♗b2 and c4. This would be a good alternative way of developing his pieces and attacking in the centre.

7	...	♗e7
8	e4	♗h7
9	♕e2	0-0
10	b3	a5!

A splendid method of gaining queenside counterplay. White's best antidote to block Black's advance is probably 11 a3 a4 12 b4.

11 a4?!

I do not like this because it weakens the b4-square, which can be occupied by a black knight.

11 ...   ♘a6!

Promptly heading for the weak square.

12 ♗b2   ♘b4

Continuing his theme of a vigorous queenside counter-offensive.

14 exd5

This capture looks suspect, since it enhances the power of Black's queen's bishop lurking on h7. I would probably have played 14 ♔h1 and then tried to advance my kingside pawns in order to whip up tactical chances in conjunction with the fianchettoed queen's bishop. (A fianchettoed bishop for White is one developed on the flank at either b2 or g2. For Black it would be a bishop mobilised on either b7 or g7.)

| 14 | ... | exd5 |
| 15 | ♘df3 | ♖e8 |

If 15 ... bxa4, then 16 ♖xa4 looks playable for White.

16	♕d2	♗d6
17	♘d4	♕b6
18	♘ef3?	

Here it is essential to play 18 axb5 cxb5 (if 18 ... c5? 19 ♘c6!) 19 ♗h3! followed by 20 ♘ef3. In that case, the white knights would mask the weakness on c2 and White would enjoy excellent control of the central squares.

| 18 | ... | bxa4 |
| 19 | bxa4 | |

If now 19 ♖xa4 then 19 ... c5!

| 19 | ... | ♞d7 |
| 20 | ♖fb1 | |

If he moves the queen's rook, then the pawn on a4 becomes weak.

| 20 | ... | ♛c7 |
| 21 | ♛c3 *(9)* | |

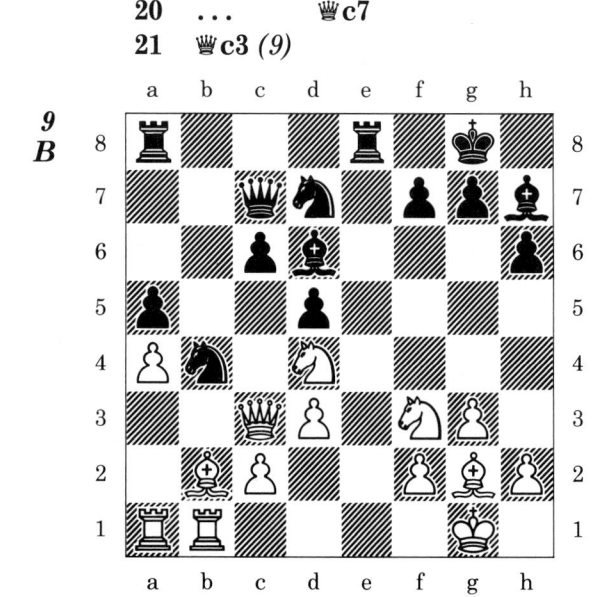

Very artificial. The threat against g7 is transparent and White's pieces are getting into an ugly tangle.

| 21 | ... | ♞e5 |
| 22 | ♞h4 | f6 |

Blocking the diagonal of White's queen and bishop and squashing any hopes Miles may have harboured of a swindle based on ♛xg7.

| 23 | ♗h3 | |

By leaving f3 unprotected, White invites a possibly unpleasant future knight check on that square. Maybe 23 ♗a3!? instead was a better idea.

| 23 | ... | ♖ab8 |
| 24 | ♞hf5 | ♗f8 |

| 25 | ♞e3 | ♛f7 |

The threat is ... c5 and ... d4.

| 26 | ♞b3 | c5! |

Things are out of control for White, since 27 ♞xc5 d4! 28 ♛xd4 ♞f3+ is hopeless.

| 27 | d4 | |

Desperation.

| 27 | ... | ♞f3+ |
| 28 | ♔f1 *(10)* | |

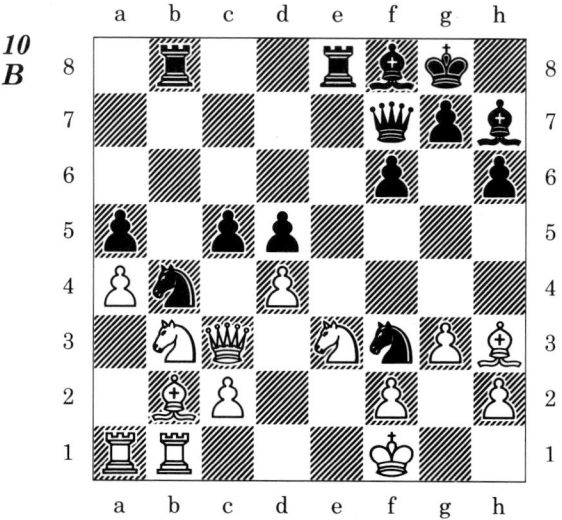

Now Short uncorks a crushing combination which knocks White's whole position out of joint.

| 28 | ... | ♞xc2! |
| 29 | ♞xc5 | |

If 29 ♞xc2 ♖xb3! 30 ♛xb3 ♞d2+ winning the queen.

29	...	♞xa1
30	♖xa1	♗xc5
	White resigns	

Both 31 ♛xc5 ♖xb2 and 31 dxc5 d4! are murderous.

17

Nigel Short (Mark Huba).

GAME THREE

White: Nigel Short
Black: Gary Kasparov
Brussels (OHRA) 1986
Sicilian Defence, Najdorf Variation

By 1986 Nigel had already earned the Grandmaster title, won the British Championship outright and competed in the World Championship Candidates tournament — the first Briton ever to do so. One of Nigel's finest efforts was his spectacular and hard-fought victory against the recently crowned World Champion, Gary Kasparov, in an international tournament in Brussels in 1986.

1	e4	c5

The Sicilian — Black's sharpest defence to 1 e4.

2	♘f3	d6
3	d4	cxd4
4	♘xd4	♘f6
5	♘c3	a6

This is the starting position line of the so-called Najdorf Variation of the Sicilian Defence — one of the most popular choices at grandmaster level and a firm favourite of the World Champion.

6	♗e3	e6
7	♕d2	b5
8	f3	♘bd7
9	g4	h6

10	0-0-0	(11)

This system has been popularised by Short and is generally known as the English Attack. The key moves for White are f3 and g4, followed by 0-0-0. Then, White will try to blast Black's king by surging forward with his kingside pawns.

10	...	♗b7
11	♗d3	♘e5
12	♖he1	♖c8
13	♔b1	♗e7

Here Black should probably react with 13

... g5. If then 14 h4 gxh4 15 ♖h1 ♘fd7 and Black has chances in this interesting position. At the moment, the bishop is not well placed on e7.

The World Champion, Gary Kasparov (Caroline Winkler).

14	h4	b4
15	♘a4 *(12)*	

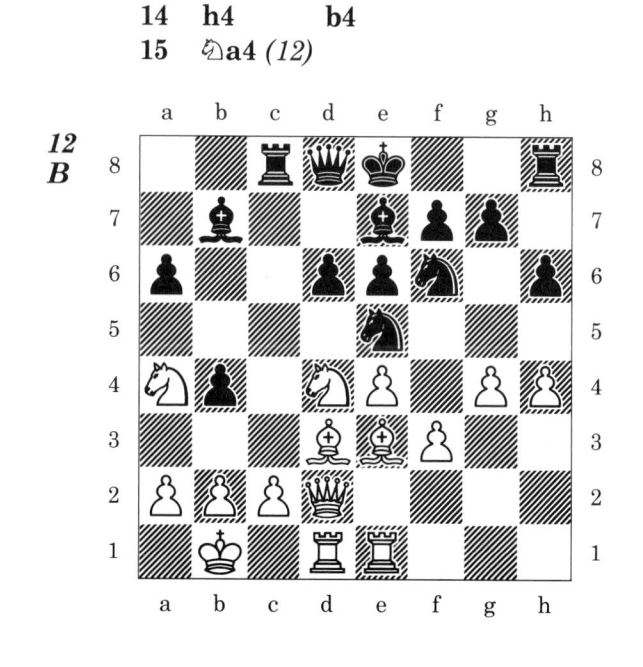

| 15 | ... | ♛a5 |

Black would like to play 15 ... d5, but 16 g5 dxe4 17 gxf6 exploits the inferior position of Black's bishop.

| 16 | b3 | ♞fd7 |
| 17 | g5 | g6 |

The best move in a difficult position. If Black does not play this White continues f3–f4 to be followed by g5–g6, instigating a massive avalanche which Black could hardly withstand.

18	f4	♞xd3
19	cxd3	hxg5
20	hxg5	d5
21	f5	(13)

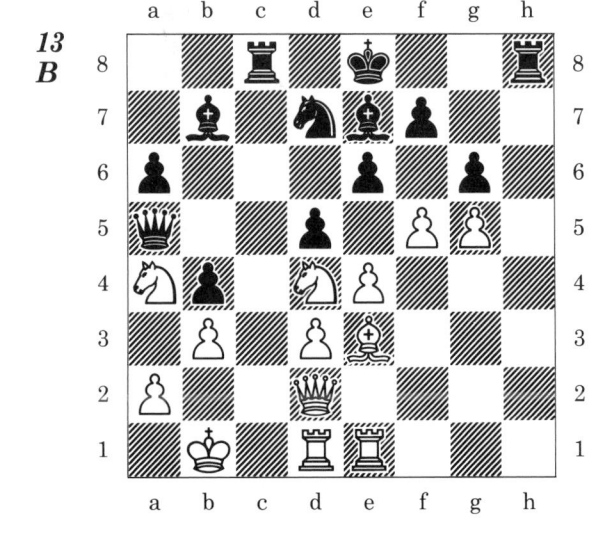

A thematic thrust which looks most promising. Nevertheless, it lets Black's queen's bishop into the action. Afterwards Kasparov said that White should have preferred 21 e5 with 22 ♖h1 to follow when sacrificial ideas of f4–f5 are in the air.

21	...	e5
22	exd5	♛xd5
23	f6	♝d6
24	♞c2	a5
25	♝a7	

An original idea, but 25 d4 might have

been better, for example 25 ... e4 26 ♝f4 intending 27 ♖h1.

25	...	♚f8
26	♞e3	♛e6
27	♞c4	♚g8
28	♞xd6	♛xd6

At last, Black has achieved level prospects. Nevertheless, the position remains tense and difficult for both sides.

29	♞b2	♖c3
30	♞c4	♛d5
31	♞e3	♛e6

A serious error. Stronger was 31 ... ♛b5 intending an eventual advance ... a5–a4 to gain counterplay.

| 32 | ♖c1 | ♛a6 |
| 33 | ♖xc3 | (14) |

Short is now forced to make an unplanned sacrifice of a piece but, luckily for him, it grants White an attack so powerful that the best that Black can hope for is a draw, and that only by extraordinarily accurate defence.

33	...	bxc3
34	♛xc3	♛xa7
35	♛c7	♛d4
36	♛xb7	♛xd3+
37	♞c2	♖h2

This looks all right for Black at the moment, but his king is permanently locked up.

> **38 ♕c8+   ♘f8?**

The only move is 38 ... ♔h7, but even so White keeps his good position after 39 ♕c6.

> **39 ♖xe5   ♖h1+**
> **40 ♔b2   ♕d2**
> **41 ♖e8!** *(15)*

Winning the knight by force.

> **41 ...   ♕d6**
> **42 ♖d8   ♕e5+**
> **43 ♔a3   ♔h7**
> **44 ♖xf8   ♕d6+**
> **45 b4   Black resigns**

A fascinating struggle, and a great win against a great opponent.

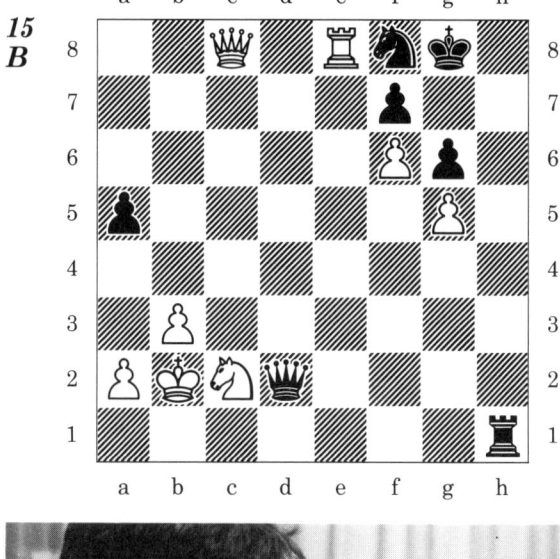

15
B

Nigel enjoys a friendly post-mortem with Gary Kasparov at Tilburg 1991 (Alain Fayard).

GAME FOUR

White: Nigel Short
Black: Gary Kasparov
London rapidplay match (6) 1987
Sicilian Defence, Najdorf Variation

Nigel's win against Gary Kasparov at Brussels was rewarded with a television match — at speed chess rates — against the World Champion in London early the following year. This unusual and exciting event was held at The Hippodrome, a famous nightspot in London, and was sponsored by London Docklands Development Corporation for broadcasting by Thames TV and Channel 4.

After trailing by four points to one in this match against Kasparov, Nigel Short struck back to take the sixth game of the Speed Chess Challenge. During the twentieth century only six British wins have been registered against reigning World Champions. And of those six Nigel Short — just 21 years old at the time — had scored no fewer than three, two of them in this match.

After the match, Kasparov claimed that within a year Short would be the main Western contender for the World Championship. This prediction was confirmed by Nigel's brilliant victory at the super-strong IBM tournament in Reykjavik the following month, although it was to take several years for Nigel to launch a successful campaign in the World Championship cycle.

1	e4	c5
2	♘f3	d6
3	d4	cxd4
4	♘xd4	♘f6

The Sicilian Defence is more of a counterattack than a defence. It has a risky reputation, but also scores a high percentage of wins. To Kasparov, it is second nature to play it.

5	♘c3	a6
6	♗e3	e6
7	f3	♘bd7
8	g4	h6

Nigel in action against the World Champion.

9   h4 (16)

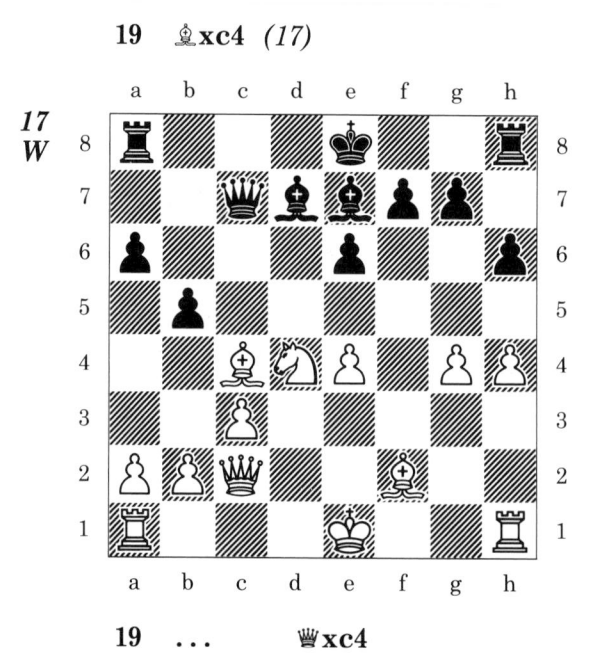

19   ♗xc4 (17)

In the second game of this match, Kasparov had continued with 9 ... b5. Now he comes up with a major improvement. It is also worth comparing the very similar opening play of the preceding game in this book.

9	...	♘e5!
10	♖g1?	

Surprised by Kasparov's innovation, Nigel goes astray. The correct course is 10 ♕e2, planning 0-0-0. After White's error, Gary immediately captures the initiative.

10	...	♕b6
11	♕c1	d5

The correct counter-measure to White's wing manoeuvres. Black strikes back in the centre.

12	♗e2	dxe4
13	♘xe4	♘xe4
14	fxe4	♗e7
15	♖h1	♗d7
16	c3	♕c7
17	♗f2	b5

Now Black has the initiative.

18	♕c2	♘c4

19	...	♕xc4

Black's 19th move is incorrect. It might have been profitably replaced with 19 ... bxc4 intending to pile up against White's position by later doubling rooks on the open b-file.

20	b3	♕c7
21	0-0-0	0-0
22	♔b1	a5
23	g5	h5
24	♖hg1	a4?

The wrong way of prosecuting his assault. More promising would have been the pawn sacrifice 24 ... b4!? 25 cxb4 ♕b7.

25	b4	♖ac8
26	♖d3	g6
27	♗g3	♕b7
28	♕e2	♖c4
29	♗e5!	

White's bishop seizes a splendid diagonal.

29	...	♖fc8
30	♕e3	♗c6
31	♖e1	a3

32 ♕f4! (18)

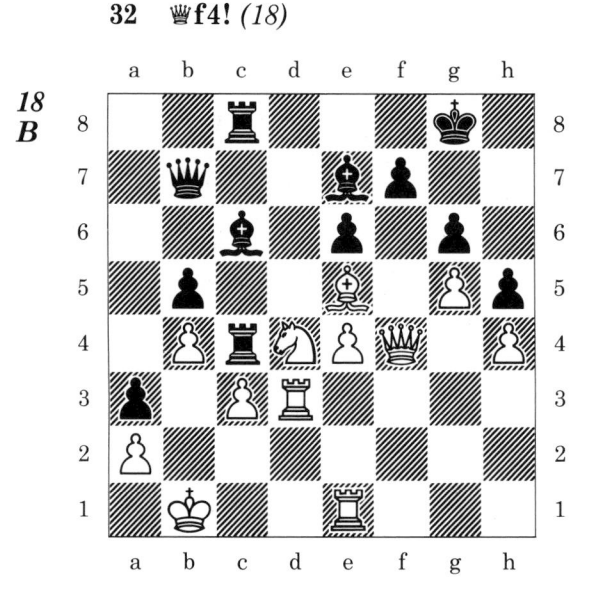

35 ♔a1!! (19)

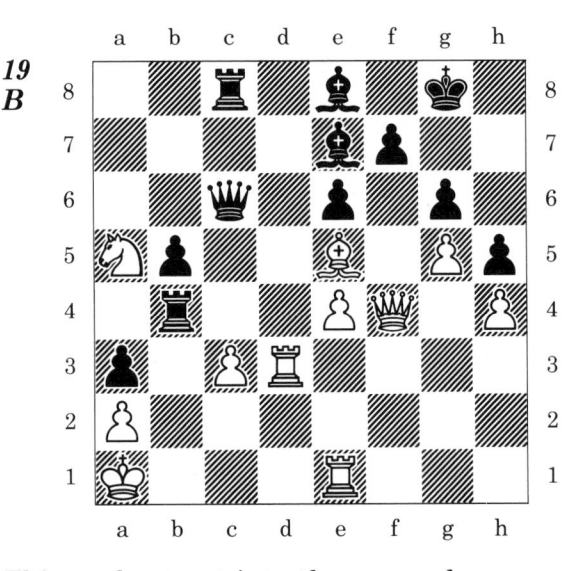

It might appear that Kasparov has a devastating sacrificial combination at his fingertips, namely 32 ... ♗xb4 33 cxb4 ♗xe4 34 ♖xe4 ♕xe4 35 ♕xe4 ♖c1 checkmate. However, the interpolation 33 ♕f6! foils all of this ingenuity and leaves Black himself facing checkmate.

32	...	♗e8
33	♘b3	♕c6
34	♘a5	♖xb4+

White appears to be crushed, since 35 cxb4 permits 35 ... ♕c2+. But Nigel has seen further than the World Champion.

This cool retreat into the corner leaves Black with his queen and rook under attack. Kasparov tries some highly ingenious last-minute sacrifices, but they are doomed to failure.

35	...	♕c5
36	cxb4	♕xb4
37	♕d2	♖c2
38	♕xb4	♗xb4

Black still has threats, but they can be refuted if White keeps his head.

39	♖d8	f6
40	♖f1	fxe5
41	♖xe8+	♔g7
42	♘b3	♗c3+
43	♔b1	♖b2+
44	♔c1	♖xb3

45 ♔c2! *(20)*

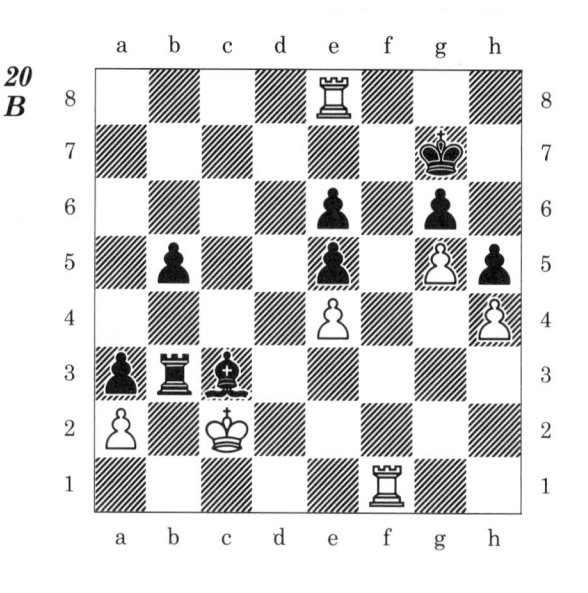

Forking Black's last remaining pieces.

Black resigns

This game is one of the most dramatic, cliff-hanging clashes in this entire collection, and shows Nigel's superb fighting spirit in tough situations.

Nigel Short and Gary Kasparov at the 1990 Immopar tournament in Paris (Caroline Winkler).

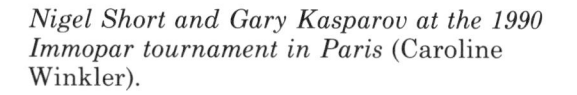

GAME FIVE

White: Nigel Short
Black: Jan Timman
KRO match (4), Hilversum 1989
Petroff Defence

Nigel qualified for the World Championship Candidates tournament for the second time in 1988. He proceeded as far as the quarter-final, but was eliminated by his friend and colleague on the England Olympic team, Grandmaster Jon Speelman. Speelman, in turn, was knocked out in the semi-final by the Dutchman, Jan Timman. This subsequent win against Timman must, therefore, have been a particularly encouraging one for Nigel. Also, it is the first foretaste in this book of the World Championship clash between Timman and Short in 1993; this would be a vital step for Short on his path to challenge Kasparov.

1	e4	e5
2	♘f3	♘f6
3	♘xe5 (21)	

21 B

The Petroff Defence, named after the nineteenth century Russian master, is a direct attempt to equalise the position by copying White's moves.

3	...	d6

Not falling into the elementary trap, 3 ... ♘xe4 4 ♕e2 ♘f6 5 ♘c6+ winning the black queen with a discovered check. This has claimed many beginners' scalps.

4	♘f3	♘xe4

Now this is safe.

5	d4	d5
6	♗d3	♗d6
7	0-0	0-0
8	c4	

The central thrust gives White some initiative, even though the position is symmetrical and looks fairly balanced.

The Dutch grandmaster Jan Timman (Mark Huba).

8	...	c6
9	cxd5	cxd5
10	♘c3	♘xc3
11	bxc3	♗g4
12	♖b1	*(22)*

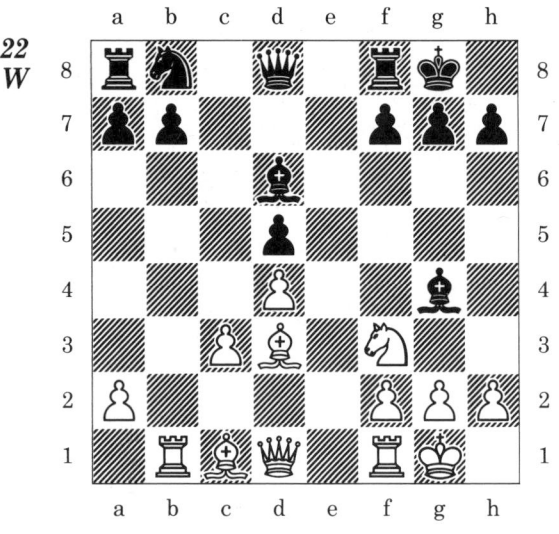

The rook on the open file is very useful.

12	...	b6

Black is provoked into a slight, but ultimately significant weakening of his queenside pawns. It would appear more natural to play 12 ... ♕c7 which performs the triple function of defending b7, attacking c3 and threatening White's pawn on h2. However, this dream move fails tactically, e.g. 12 ... ♕c7 13 ♗xh7+ ♔xh7 14 ♘g5+ ♔g8 15 ♕xg4 with advantage to White.

13	♖b5	

The rook swings into action.

13	...	♗c7
14	c4	dxc4

This position had occurred before in Short's games. Timman now produces a new idea which, at first sight, appears to lose material. In fact, Black's defence is based on complex tactics and comes close to succeeding.

15	♗e4	♘c6

If now 16 ♗xc6, then 16 ... ♕d6 threatens both ... ♕xc6 and ... ♗xf3 followed by ... ♕xh2 mate. Short prefers to prosecute his kingside offensive.

16	♖g5	♗xf3

This move commits Black to the loss of the exchange, but he hopes to gain ample compensation in terms of central control.

17	♕xf3	♕d6
18	♖g3	♘xd4
19	♕g4	*(23)*

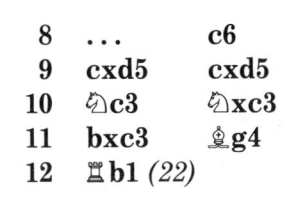

29

This is the key move. White threatens mate on g7 as well as the black rook on a8.

19	...	g6
20	♗xa8	♖xa8
21	♖d1	♖d8
22	♔f1	*(24)*

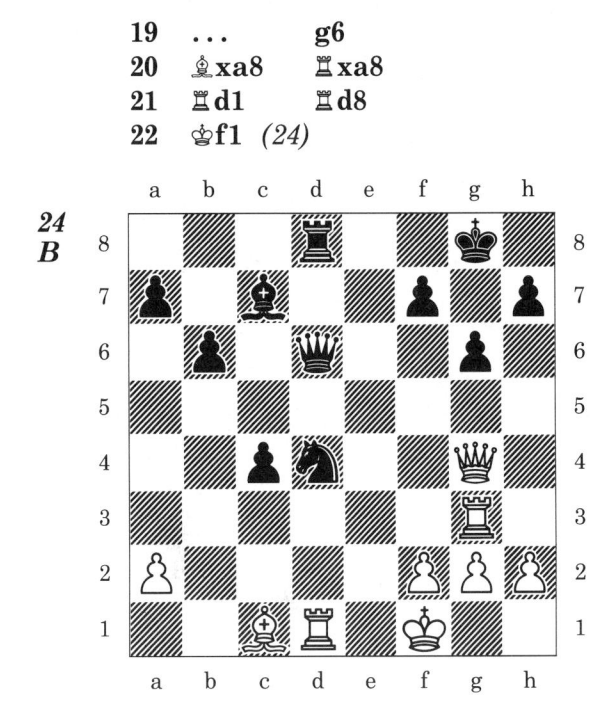

This move is excellent. Black suffers from a serious pin on the d-file which cannot sensibly be broken. The point of 22 ♔f1 is to prevent Black lifting the pin by means of a knight check on e2 or f3.

| 22 | ... | ♛d5 |
| 23 | ♖e3 | *(25)* |

The crisis has been reached. White threatens 24 ♖xd4 ♛xd4 25 ♖e8+ ♔g7 26 ♛xd4 ♖xd4 27 ♗b2, so in order to ward off this horror, as well as other variations based on the augmentation of the pin by ♗b2, Timman must irrevocably weaken the fortifications surrounding his king.

23	...	f5
24	♛h4	f4
25	♖e7	h5
26	♛f6	**Black resigns**

Suddenly Black is helpless.

A very sharp win against a top-notch opponent, one whose name will feature again in this book.

Nigel in conversation with Judit and Sofia Polgar (Helmut Schneider).

GAME SIX

White: Nigel Short
Black: Robert Hübner
World Championship Interzonal, Manila 1990
Ruy Lopez, Worrall Attack

Once again, having won team silver medals for England in the Olympics of 1984, 1986 and 1988, Nigel set off in 1990 on the round of qualifying for the individual World Championship. This wonderfully elegant win against Germany's undisputed top grandmaster, was a vitally important stepping-stone on the road to qualification from the Interzonal tournament to the Candidates matches.

	1	e4	e5
	2	♘f3	♘c6
	3	♗b5	*(26)*

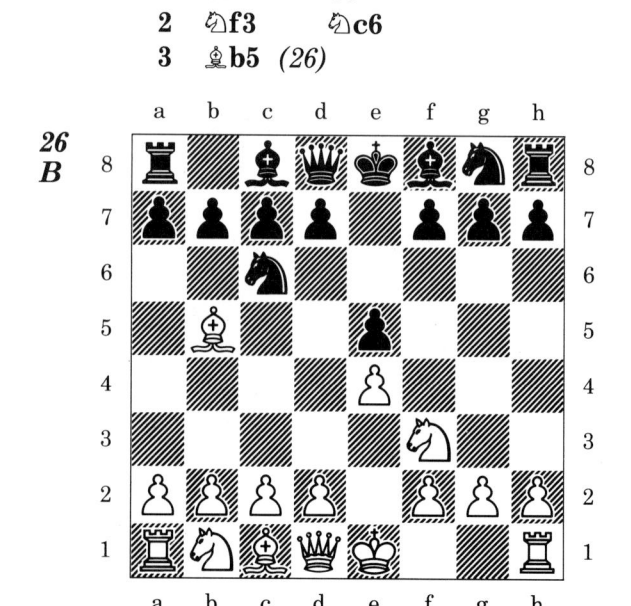

The Ruy Lopez, invented in the sixteenth century in Spain, is one of the oldest and most respected openings. It is a particular favourite with Nigel, who has scored many excellent wins with it.

	3	...	a6
	4	♗a4	♘f6

	5	0-0	♗e7
	6	♕e2	

6 ♕e2 (the Worrall Attack) is a Nigel Short speciality and is a good alternative to the usual 6 ♖e1. Pay attention to this move. It crops up later in this book in one of the games against Anatoly Karpov.

	6	...	b5
	7	♗b3	0-0
	8	c3	d5

A vigorous way of inaugurating a central counterattack against White's somewhat unusual system. The alternative is 8 ... d6 9 d4 ♗g4 10 ♖d1 ♕c8 11 a4 which was played in the game Chandler–Olafsson, Hastings 1990/91.

	9	d3	♗b7
	10	♖e1	♖e8
	11	♘bd2	♗f8

12 a3 *(27)*

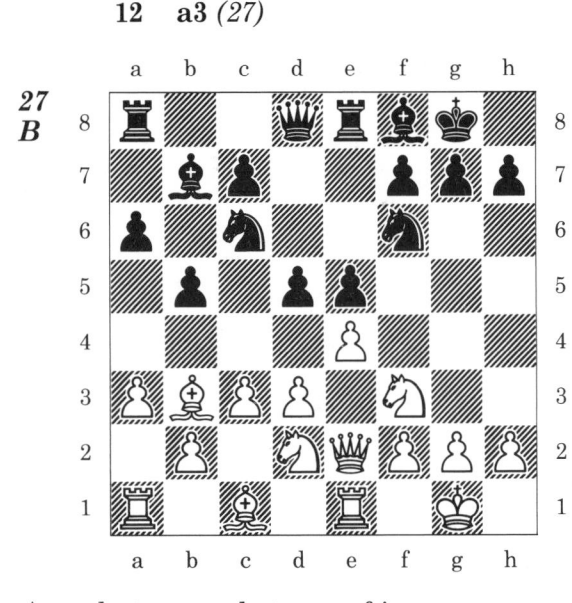

A modest move, but one of immense importance. The subtle point of White's play is to ensure at all costs that the white king's bishop has a haven on a2 and cannot be driven from the important attacking a2–g8 diagonal by an untimely ... ♞a5 from Black.

12	...	♞a5
13	♗a2	c5
14	b4	♞c6

One small slip in the implementation of his opening defensive strategy, and the German grandmaster suddenly finds himself mercilessly harried by a sequence of exceedingly accurate tactical play from Short. The correct defensive method resides in 14 ... cxb4 without any hesitation, for example, 15 cxb4 ♞c6 16 ♗b2 a5 or 15 axb4 ♞c6 16 exd5 ♞xd5 17 ♞e4 ♛d7 with sufficient counterplay in both cases.

15 exd5

Quite often it is suspect to give up the centre in this fashion, but in this case the exchange is justified since White can create specific threats radiating through the light-squared diagonals towards the sensitive points in the Black position on d5, f7 and h7.

15	...	♞xd5
16	♞e4	cxb4
17	♞fg5! *(28)*	

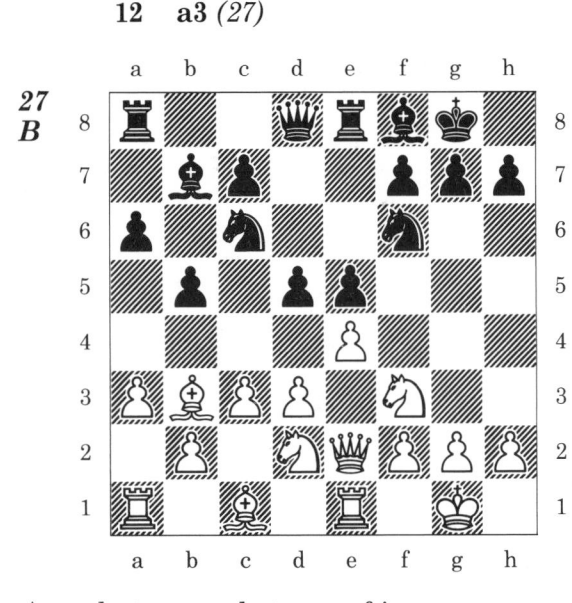

A horrid surprise for Black who must have been expecting the stereotyped recapture 17 axb4. Suddenly, White unveils menacing attacking schemes which could result in immediate disaster for Black were he not to defend with utmost caution. For example, if now 17 ... ♛d7 18 ♛h5 h6 19 ♞xf7 ♛xf7 20 ♛xf7+ ♚xf7 21 ♗xd5+ ♚g6 22 axb4 with a winning advantage. Alternatively, from diagram 28, 17 ... ♜e7 18 ♞xh7 ♚xh7 19 ♛h5+ ♚g8 20 ♞g5 ♞f6 21 ♗xf7+ ♜xf7 22 ♛xf7+ ♚h8 23 ♛xb7 again with a winning advantage.

17	...	h6
18	♛f3	

White's queen swoops into action as a decisive reinforcement to the light-squared onslaught. If Black now seeks to defend with 18 ... ♜e7 then 19 ♞c5 wins.

18	...	hxg5
19	♞xg5	♛f6

20 ♕xd5 *(29)*

The white queen is truly impressive on this centralised post.

20 ...   ♘d8

If here 20 ... ♖e7 then 21 ♕e4 g6 22 ♕h4 ♕g7 23 axb4 with decisive advantage.

21 ♕d7   ♗c6
22 ♕h3   ♗c5

A somewhat better defence is afforded by 22 ... ♕h6 but, in fact, Black's position is already shattered.

23 d4   b3
24 ♗xb3   ♗b6
25 ♕h7+   ♔f8
26 ♖a2

The most efficient manner of doubling his rooks on the all important e-file.

26 ...   ♗d7

Nigel at the 1991 Tilburg tournament (Alain Fayard).

27 ♖ae2   ♗f5 *(30)*

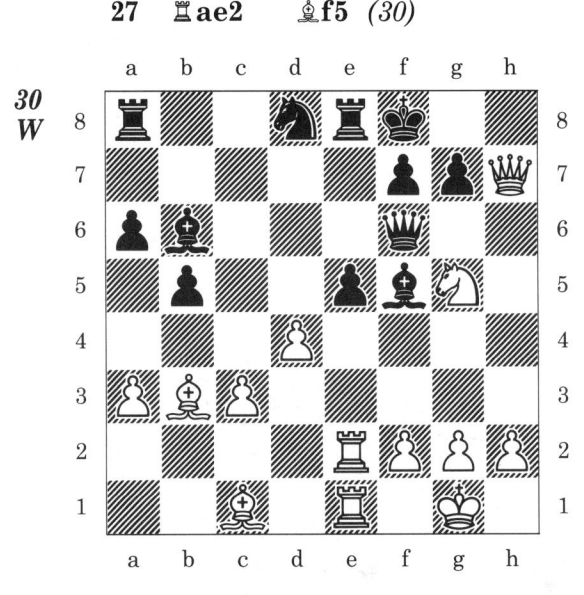

It might appear that Black is constructing some sort of defence, but White's next move swiftly dissolves the mirage.

28 ♖xe5   ♖xe5

If at once 28 ... ♗xh7 then 29 ♖xe8 is checkmate. Ultimately, Black is forced to capture the white queen but his reward is a completely hopeless endgame.

29 ♖xe5   ♗xh7
30 ♘xh7+   ♔g8
31 ♘xf6+   gxf6
32 ♖e8+   ♔g7 *(31)*

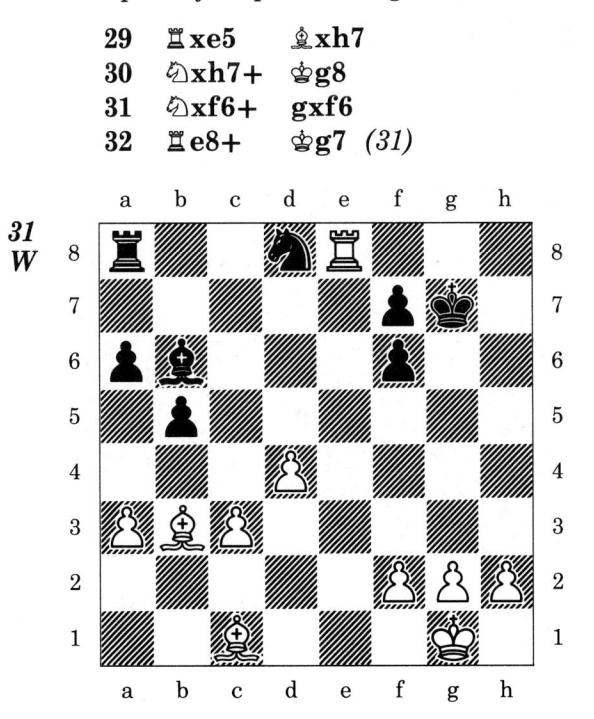

Black's position is shattered and paralysed.

33	h4	♖c8
34	♗d2	♗a5
35	g4	♗xc3
36	♖xd8	♖xd8
37	♗xc3	♖c8

Now White has a decisive material advantage.

38	♗d2	♖d8
39	d5	♖a8
40	♗a5	♔f8
41	d6	**Black resigns**

Besieged by photographers during the Candidates match with Boris Gelfand (Helmut Schneider).

GAME SEVEN

White: Nigel Short
Black: Boris Gelfand
World Championship Candidates Quarter-Final match (3), Brussels 1991
Sicilian Defence, Grand Prix Attack

Nigel, now the highest-ranked English grandmaster ever, became only the second British player to qualify for the World Chess Championship semi-finals. (The first was Jon Speelman in 1989 who, ironically, had defeated Short himself in the quarter-final stage, a result which Nigel reversed in the eighth-final in early 1991.) Nigel achieved this by comprehensively crushing his opponent in the quarter-finals in Brussels, the higher-rated Soviet grandmaster, Boris Gelfand. It was the most turbulent of the four concurrent quarter-finals, with only two of the eight games ending as draws and with the outcome uncertain until the final move of the final game.

By winning, Short went on to join the Dutch grandmaster Jan Timman and living legend Anatoly Karpov, World Champion for a decade from 1975 to 1985, in the semi-finals. The fourth member of the victorious quadrumvirate was Artur Yusupov who beat his compatriot, Vassily Ivanchuk, in a speed chess play-off after their 4–4 tie. The pairings for the semi-finals pitted Short against Karpov and Yusupov against Timman. Nigel thus faced the most difficult challenge of his career.

	1	e4	c5
	2	♘c3	

This is a subtle move order. In the first place, it keeps Black guessing as to White's intentions (since Black can hardly prevent White from playing ♘f3 and d4 if he wants to, at some later stage). It also prevents Black from playing an early ... d5 defence (which more or less completely equalises if White plays 2 f4).

	2	...	d6
	3	f4	♘c6
	4	♘f3	g6
	5	♗c4	(32)

32
B

A model of concentration (Helmut Schneider).

A somewhat rustic-seeming development for the bishop, the more so since it would appear that the pressure against f7 can be blunted by means of ... e6. Nevertheless, this line contains more than a drop of poison and is known in England as the Grand Prix Attack, due to its popularity on the weekend tournament circuit.

5	...	♗g7
6	0-0	e6
7	d3	

Here, White has the chance to play the dangerous pawn sacrifice f5. In this case Black is obliged to take it. Having already expended a tempo on ... d6, Black would be a whole move down on an already razor-sharp variation if he declined the pawn. One possibility is 7 f5 exf5 8 d3 ♘ge7 9 ♕e1 h6 10 exf5 ♗xf5 11 g4 ♗xg4 12 ♗xf7+ ♔xf7 13 ♘e5+ ♔g8 14 ♘xg4 ♘d4 15 ♕f2 ♘df5 when Black eventually won in Hellers–Gelfand, Novi Sad Olympiad 1990. This shows that Gelfand was familiar with the

Grand Prix Attack, though it probably did not figure highly on his agenda of theory as preparation for his Candidates quarter-final match.

7	...	♞ge7
8	♛e1	

Black's next move, even though it is quite natural, is probably a theoretical novelty in this precise position. The main conclusion to be drawn from this is that the position after 8 ♛e1 is simply not very well charted at international level.

8	...	♞d4

The alternative is 8 ... 0-0, to castle Black's king into safety as speedily as possible.

9	♞xd4	cxd4
10	♞e2	0-0
11	♗b3	♞c6
12	♗d2	d5

Inviting White to seal the centre ...

13	e5

... which he gladly does, shutting in Black's king's bishop at the same time.

13	...	f6 (33)

Not unnaturally, Gelfand wishes to blast a path for his king's bishop to get back into the game, but this thrust necessarily weakens the dark squares surrounding his king, in particular granting White a beckoning outpost on e5 for his knight. It is fascinating how often we see this kind of motif in Short's games — an advanced White spearhead pawn on e5 being challenged by Black's ... f6. Short nearly always responds with exf6 and then proceeds to exploit the weaknesses Black tends to obtain, on e6 specifically and on the kingside in general.

14	exf6	♗xf6
15	♔h1!	

A very fine and far-sighted move. Not only does White tuck his king away into safety at the edge of the board, he also prepares the strategic manoeuvre ♞g1–f3–e5 to profit from Black's 13th move.

15	...	a5
16	a4	♛d6
17	♞g1	♗d7
18	♞f3	♞b4
19	♛f2	♛c5
20	♗c3	(34)

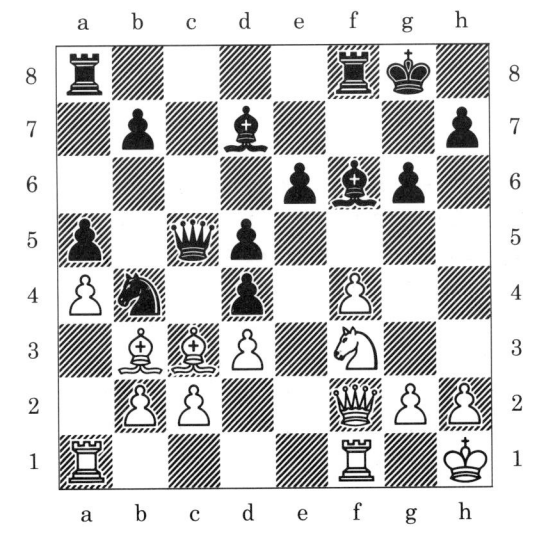

Action from the Short-Gelfand match (Helmut Schneider).

I found this move very surprising, just because, optically I suppose, the c3-square seems forbidden territory to the white bishop. But of course, it is immune from capture due to the pin against Black's queen.

| 20 | ... | ♘c6 |
| 21 | ♖ae1 | b6 |

Defending his queen and thus forcing the white bishop to retreat.

| 22 | ♗d2 | ♘b4 |
| 23 | ♕g3 | (35) |

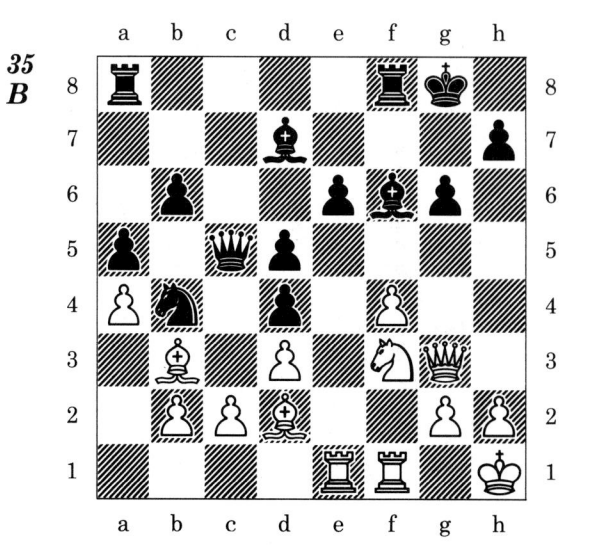

Storm clouds are gathering around the black king but Gelfand seems curiously oblivious to the coming tempest. His next move, a continuation of his own attack on the queenside, is unpardonably careless. It is high time to think of defence, for example by ferrying over an extra piece to the kingside by means of 23 ... ♖ae8.

| 23 | ... | b5 |
| 24 | f5! | |

This blow comes with all the greater force for having been delayed. Black's position is now so disorganised that White's attack almost plays itself.

| 24 | ... | exf5 |

If 24 ... bxa4 then 25 fxe6 or 25 fxg6 both look extremely dangerous for Black, e.g. 24 ... bxa4 25 fxg6 axb3 26 gxh7+ ♔h8 27 ♘e5 ♗xe5 28 ♕xe5+ with a mating attack.

| 25 | ♘e5 | ♗e8 |

Abject retreat, but if 25 ... ♗xe5 26 ♕xe5 ♖ae8 27 ♗xb4! and whichever way Black recaptures he is doomed to suffer intolerable levels of material loss.

| 26 | axb5 | ♕xb5 |
| 27 | ♖xf5 | ♔h8 (36) |

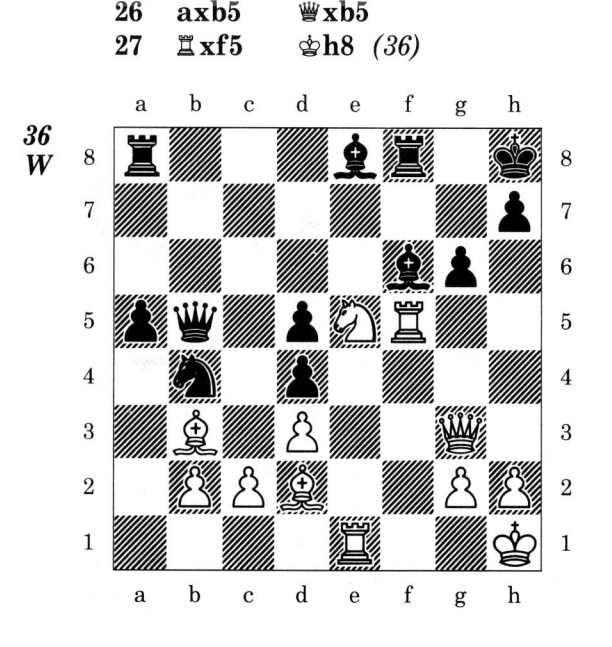

36 W

Nigel's next move is the *coup de grâce* which knocks out the defender of Black's dark squares and leaves Black's king totally exposed to a crushing dark-square mating attack.

28	♖xf6	♖xf6
29	♘g4	♖f5
30	♘h6	♖h5
31	♕f4 (37)	**Black resigns**

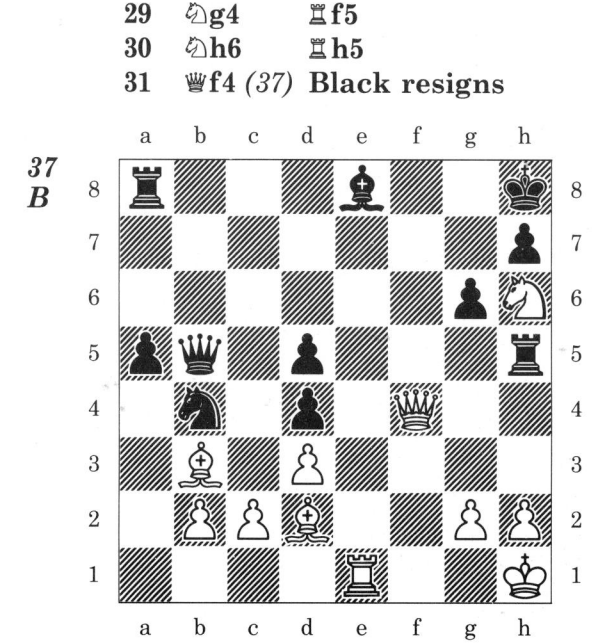

37 B

White's threats against the black king are utterly overwhelming.

GAME EIGHT

White: Nigel Short
Black: Jan Timman
Tilburg (Interpolis) 1991
Alekhine Defence

As we know, Nigel was later to face Timman in the final match of the World Championship qualifying competition in January 1993. This was the last hurdle for both of them, before one went on to meet Kasparov. Clashes between Short and Timman are almost always epics which offer great value. This battle at the super-strong Tilburg event was no exception.

	1	e4	♘f6

Invented by Alexander Alekhine — World Champion in the 1920s, 1930s and 1940s — this defence is both risky and provocative. It encourages White to rage forward with his centre pawns; they may then become a source of strength or, if Black has his way, an over-exposed target.

	2	e5	♘d5
	3	d4	d6
	4	♘f3	g6
	5	♗c4	♘b6 (38)

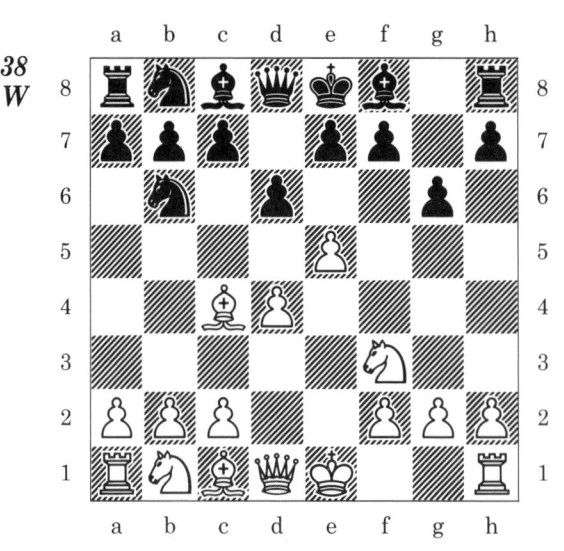

Alekhine's Defence is quite an onerous burden against Short, since he is so good at exploiting a solid advantage in space.

	6	♗b3	♗g7
	7	♕e2!	

Efficiently reinforcing the strongpoint on the e5-square.

	7	...	♘c6
	8	0-0	0-0
	9	h3	a5!?

9 ... ♞a5 is the alternative.

10	a4	dxe5
11	dxe5	♞d4
12	♞xd4	♛xd4
13	♖e1	e6 *(39)*

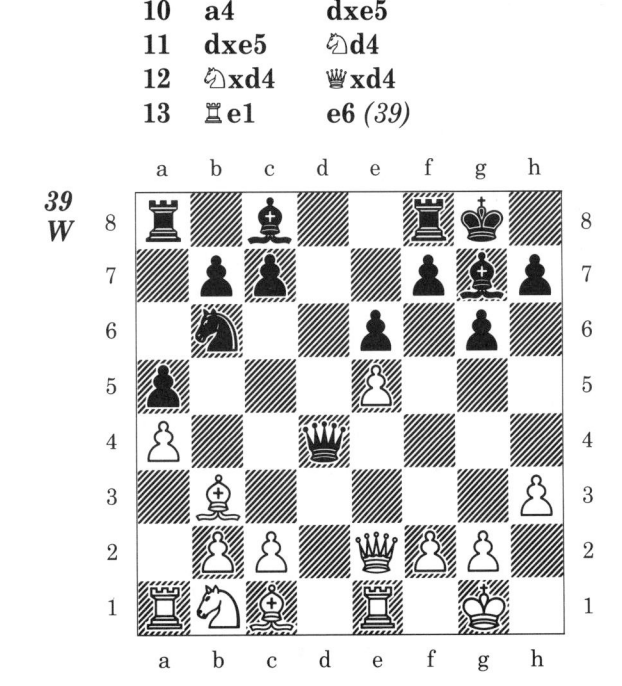

39 W

It is clear that Black's opening has not been satisfactory. His queen roams exposed around the board, the dark squares near his king are weak, and he will have trouble developing his queenside pieces, especially the queen's bishop.

| 14 | ♞d2 | ♞d5 |

According to Short himself this is a new move, but it is scarcely a great improvement on the 14 ... ♝d7 played by Michael Hennigan against Short in the British Championship at Swansea 1987. Black's position is cramped and his kingside weak, so to quote Nigel Short himself from his column in the *Daily Telegraph*: 'It is hard to imagine what Timman had in mind by repeating all this.'

| 15 | ♞f3 | ♛c5 |
| 16 | ♛e4 | ♛b4 |

Preventing ♛h4 and offering a pawn sacrifice. If now 17 ♝xd5 exd5 18 ♛xd5

then 18 ... ♝e6 gives Black a pleasant game.

| 17 | ♝c4 | ♞b6 |
| 18 | b3! *(40)* | |

40 B

An inspired conception. Conventional wisdom dictates that one should not surrender the bishop pair nor allow one's pawns to be shattered. Nigel breaks both rules in order to augment his dominance of the dark squares. The threat is now ♝a3, winning material.

| 18 | ... | ♞xc4 |
| 19 | bxc4 | |

For the small price of ruptured pawns, White has seized the initiative. 20 ♝a3, winning the exchange, is threatened.

19	...	♖e8
20	♖d1	♛c5
21	♛h4	b6
22	♝e3	♛c6

Nigel in action against the veteran Viktor Korchnoi at the 1991 Tilburg event (Alain Fayard).

23 ♗h6 ♝h8 (41)

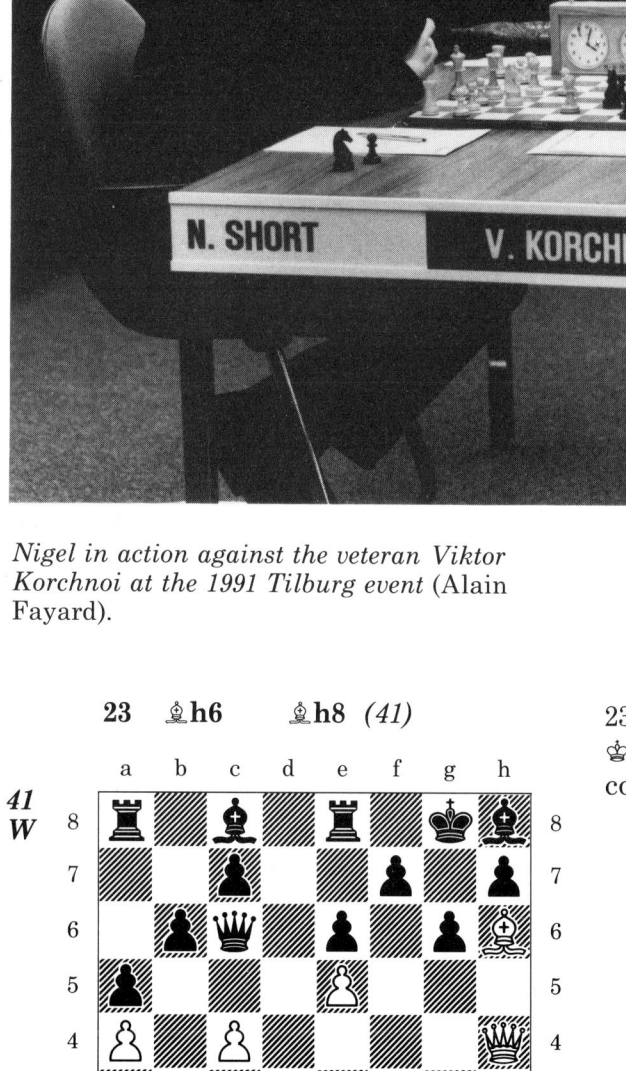

23 ... ♝b7 24 ♗xg7 ♚xg7 25 ♕f6+ ♚g8 26 ♖d4 leaves Black devoid of counterplay.

24 ♖d8 ♝b7
25 ♖ad1 ♝g7

The threat was 26 ♕e7 followed by ♖xa8 and ♖d8.

26	♖8d7	♖f8
27	♗xg7	♔xg7
28	♖1d4	♖ae8
29	♕f6+	♔g8
30	h4	h5 (42)

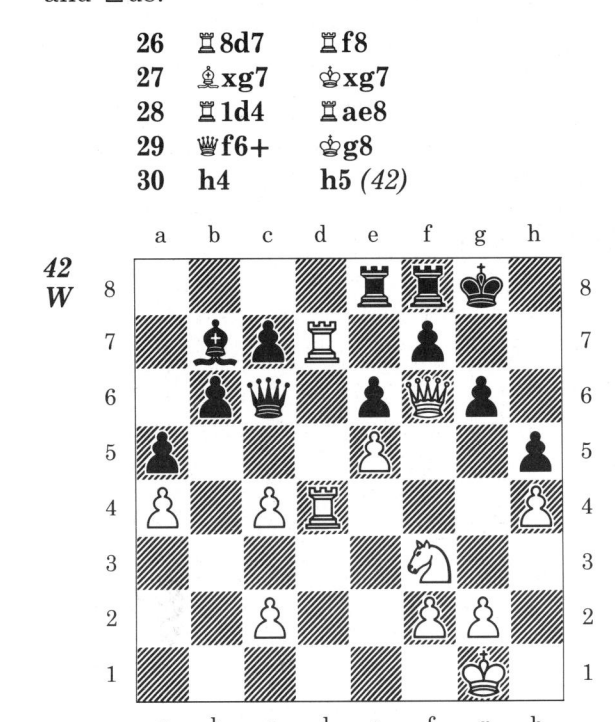

42
W

White dominates the d-file and has complete control of the dark-square terrain around Black's king. His problem, though, is that his knight cannot join the attack in view of Black's threats along the a8–h1 diagonal. Therefore Nigel activates his last passive piece, the king.

31 ♔h2!

The start of a plan of quite mind-boggling audacity. Timman fails to realise what is coming and therefore misses his only chance, 31 ... ♗c8. But as Nigel points out, 31 ... ♗c8 runs into the highly imaginative 32 g4!! ♗xd7 33 gxh5 gxh5 34 ♕g5+ with a mating attack. Nevertheless, Black can still force White to play accurately for his win after 31 ... ♗c8 32 g4 hxg4 33 ♘g5 g3+ 34 ♔xg3 ♗xd7 35 ♔h2!! ♕xa4 36 h5 gxh5 37 ♕h6 ♕xc2 38 ♘e4. A superb variation.

31	...	♖c8

Now, after this weak response, Black is utterly helpless against the spectacular and inexorable advance of the white king.

32	♔g3	♖ce8
33	♔f4	♗c8
34	♔g5! (43)	**Black resigns**

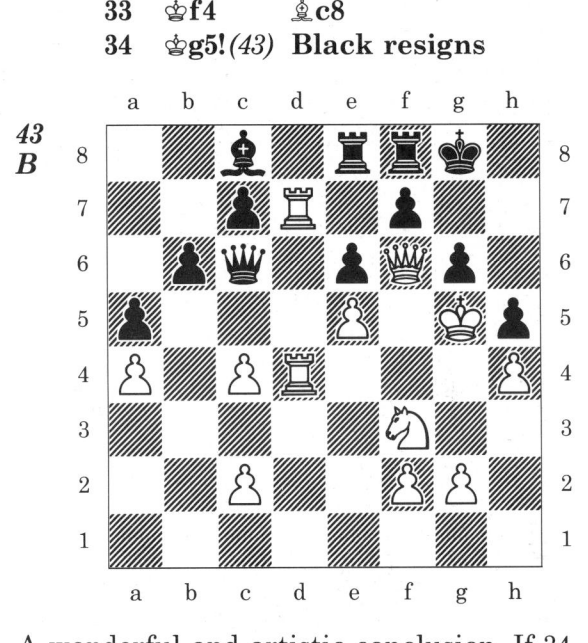

43
B

A wonderful and artistic conclusion. If 34 ... ♔h7 35 ♕xg6+ or 34 ... ♗xd7 35 ♔h6, imprisoning the black king and threatening unavoidably 36 ♕g7 mate. One of the most original finishes on record.

Analysis with the World Champion (Alain Fayard).

GAME NINE

White: Nigel Short
Black: Anatoly Karpov
World Championship Candidates Semi-Final match (8), Linares 1992
Ruy Lopez, Worrall Attack

Nigel Short's historic World Championship semi-final triumph against the former champion, Anatoly Karpov, has been covered in great detail in the Introduction. No British player has ever performed so well at this level of the World Championship. One has to cast back to the days of Howard Staunton, in the mid-1840s, to find a parallel British success. But in those days, of course, no official championship was recognised.

By general consent, the eighth game of the match was the most outstanding of all. Short employed a little-known variation of his favourite Ruy Lopez opening. At first, he appeared to be concentrating his efforts exclusively against some vulnerable points in Black's queenside fortifications. Ultimately, though, this was all revealed as a clever feint. Nigel's true intentions, which crystallised with cataclysmic fury around the 30th move, were to concentrate on and destroy the shaky residence of the black king. On the 36th move, faced with inevitable checkmate, Karpov extended his hand in a gesture of forlorn resignation. British fans at last began to believe that Nigel could truly win the match.

1	e4	e5
2	♘f3	♘c6
3	♗b5	a6
4	♗a4	♘f6
5	0-0	♗e7
6	♕e2 *(44)*	

44
B

The Worrall Attack, which we have already seen in Nigel's game against Robert Hübner, is a refreshing change from the standard 6 ♖e1, which has been analysed out almost *ad nauseam*. The queen move, which was a favourite of the great World Champion, Alexander Alekhine, is more than logical, in that it frees the white king's rook to slide to

d1 in support of the central advance c3 and d4.

In action against the former World Champion Anatoly Karpov at Linares (Alain Fayard).

6	...	b5
7	♗b3	0-0
8	c3	d6

In the Short–Hübner game, Black played 8 ... d5 9 d3 ♗b7 (9 ... d4 10 ♘bd2 ♗c5 11 ♗c2 ♗b6 12 ♘b3 ♗g4 was tried by Karpov in the sixth game of this match, but is also proved insufficient) 10 ♖e1 ♖e8 11 ♘bd2 ♗f8, but did not entirely solve the problem of the opening. Short went on to win in 41 moves. (See game 6 in this collection.)

| 9 | d4 | ♗g4 |
| 10 | ♖d1 | exd4 |

This central exchange increases White's control of terrain, but on the other hand

Black hopes thereby to activate his minor pieces.

11	cxd4	d5
12	e5	♘e4
13	a4	bxa4

A further exchange in the same vein as his tenth move, but it seems to me that Black's queenside now becomes too exposed and that 13 ... b4 would have been somewhat superior. A possible

48

continuation then, is 14 a5 ♗h4 15 ♗e3 ♘e7 with the idea of ... ♘f5.

14	♗xa4	♘b4
15	h3	♗h5
16	♘c3	♗g6
17	♗e3	♖b8
18	♘a2 (45)	

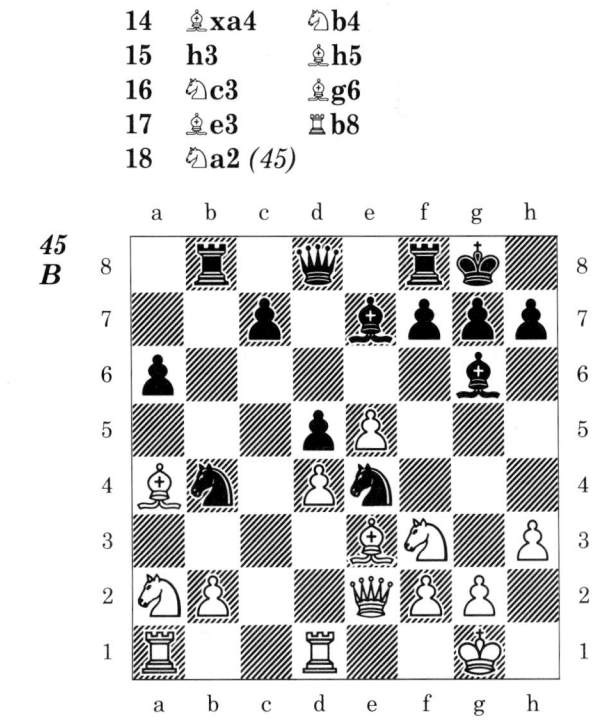

45 B

A star move, challenging one of Black's most active pieces.

18	...	c5

This thrust leaves Black with weak pawns on the a- and d-files. However, Black's hand is more or less forced, since White was threatening the simple ♖dc1 when Black has a permanent wound on the open c-file in the shape of his enfeebled and backward pawn.

19	dxc5	♘xc5
20	♘xb4	♖xb4
21	♗c6	♕b6

The only way to maintain material parity.

22	♗xd5	♖xb2

23	♕c4 (46)	

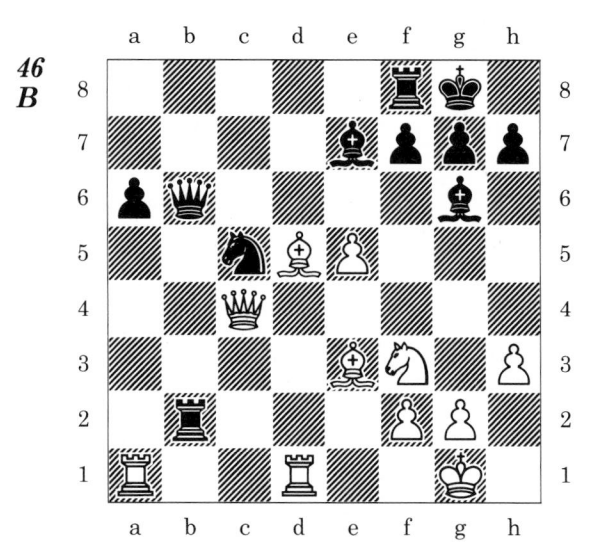

46 B

Establishing an unpleasant pin against Black's knight on c5. If now 23 ... ♖b4 then 24 ♕c1 maintains the pin. Black cannot free himself after 23 ... ♖b4 24 ♕c1 with 24 ... ♕b5 on account of 25 ♘d4. Also, after 23 ... ♖b4 24 ♕c3 would be very strong.

23	...	♖c2

Black has no choice if he wants to rescue his knight on c5, but after this move White exploits the exposed situation of the black rook to gain time for a fresh attack.

24	♕g4	♕c7
25	♘d4	♖c3
26	♘c6	♖e8
27	♗d4	♖c2
28	♘b4	

The ultimate humiliation. Black's wandering rook is now trapped and has no safe square within the heart of White's camp.

28	...	♖d8

Making the best of a bad job.

29	♘xc2	♗xc2

30 e6 (47)

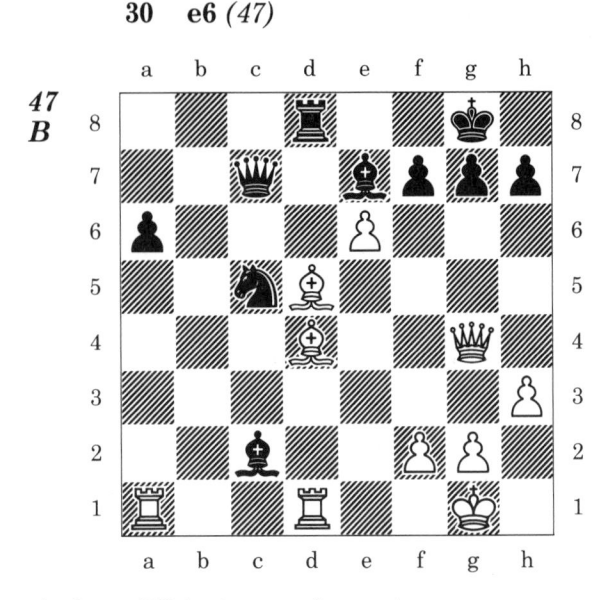

At last, White's true intentions are revealed. Black's king has been his target all along. White threatens ♕xg7 checkmate and if 30 ... f6 then 31 ♗xf6 ♗xf6 32 e7+ ♔h8 33 exd8(♕)+ ♕xd8 34 ♖ac1 ♗xd1 35 ♕xd1 with a decisive material advantage.

30	...	♗f8
31	exf7+	♔h8
32	♖e1 (48)	

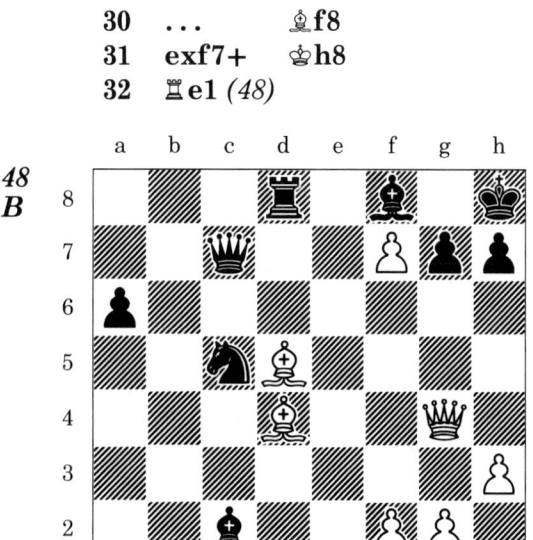

Perhaps Black had been relying on playing 32 ... ♖xd5 in this position, but in that case, Short would have available the brilliant denouement 33 ♕xg7+ ♗xg7 34 ♖e8 checkmate.

32	...	♗g6
33	♖e8	♖xe8
34	fxe8(♕)	♗xe8
35	♗xc5	♗xc5
36	♕e6	**Black resigns**

Black has no defence to ♕g8+. A magnificent game.

The 1991 Speelman-Short Candidates match graphically illustrates the tension of the big occasion (Mark Huba).

GAME TEN

White: Nigel Short
Black: Anatoly Karpov
World Championship Candidates Semi-Final match (10), Linares 1992
Sicilian Defence, Richter–Rauzer Attack

Here we discuss the historic tenth and final game of Nigel Short's match against Anatoly Karpov. It should be remembered that Nigel needed only a draw in this game to ensure his qualification, while Karpov had to win to level the scores and prolong the match into sudden death rapidplay tie-breaks. It was, therefore, a sporting gesture by Karpov to play on to the death, when a more supine character might have offered a draw when things were looking grim, just to minimise the margin of overall defeat.

In saluting Nigel's tremendous victory in this match, one must not forget the role played by Karpov. He was undisputed World Champion for a decade from 1975 to 1985 and for almost 20 years he has been either number one or number two on the world ranking list. Karpov's defeat in Linares, his first in matchplay to anyone other than Gary Kasparov, marks the passing of an era.

	1	e4	c5

Karpov has a curious relationship with the Sicilian, which is, in fact, Black's most popular, if most risky, defence to 1 e4. Kasparov's repeated use of it against Karpov himself eventually drove Karpov away from playing 1 e4 when he is White, and he now invariably chooses 1 d4. However, when Black, Karpov clearly, deep down, shares Capablanca's view that the Sicilian 'leaves Black's game full of holes'. But if you want to win, the Sicilian is really the best choice. Another view on the Sicilian was that expressed by Victor Korchnoi who said: 'Playing the Sicilian is like starting a boxing match before climbing into the ring.' I cannot recall when Karpov last utilised the Sicilian for an important game.

2	♘f3	♘c6
3	d4	cxd4
4	♘xd4	♘f6
5	♘c3	d6
6	♗g5	e6
7	♕d2	♗e7
8	0-0-0	0-0
9	♘b3	a6
10	♗xf6	

An excellent choice. If now 10 ... ♗xf6 11 ♕xd6 ♕b6 12 ♕c5 and Black cannot possibly win. Given the match situation, Black must recapture with the pawn, which in turn gives White dangerous attacking chances against the exposed black king.

10	...	gxf6
11	h4!	(49)

Nigel shares a joke with his second, Lubomir Kavalek (Sabine Kaufman).

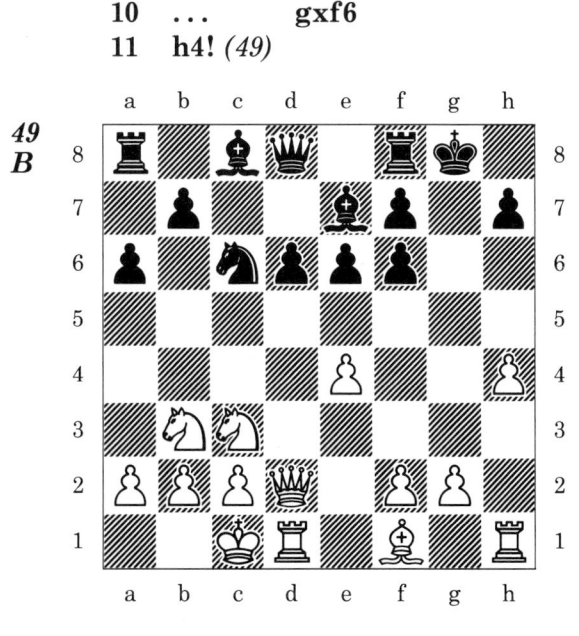

49
B

Setting the tone for the game. Although Nigel only needed a draw, the correct psychology in such situations is always to play as ruthlessly as possible for the win. Anything else tends to induce pacifist tendencies which can be fatal.

11	...	♔h8

11 ... b5 12 g4 b4 13 ♘e2 ♔h8 14 g5 a5 15 ♘ed4 ♘xd4 16 ♘xd4 was seen in van der Wiel–Piket, Lyon Zonal 1990.

12	g4	b5
13	g5	b4
14	♘a4!	

Another bold move. On this square the knight is exposed to attack. On the other hand, the knight blocks any ambitions

52

Black might have harboured of advancing his a-pawn. Furthermore, the knight may jump into b6 with advantage, which, in fact, is just what happens.

14	...	♖g8
15	f4	♖b8
16	♔b1	♗f8
17	♗e2 *(50)*	

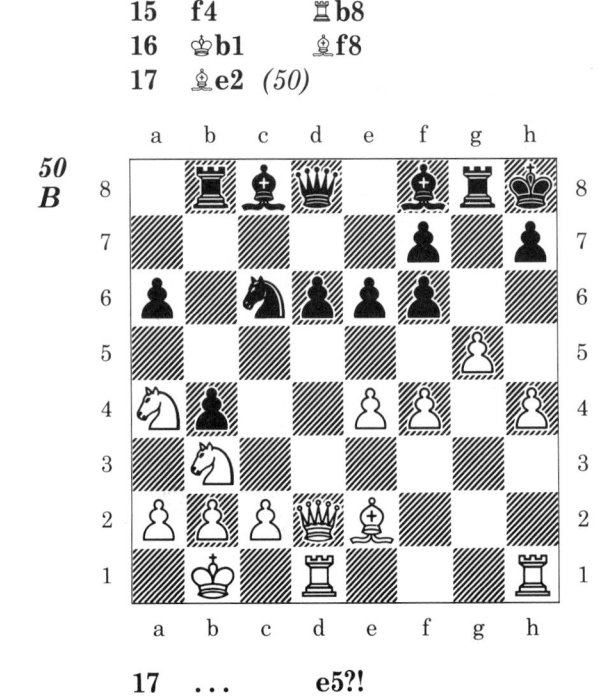

17	...	e5?!

From a strategic point of view, this move is hopeless. The entire complex of light squares in and around Black's camp is weakened at a stroke and beyond repair. Nevertheless, the laudable point behind Black's 17th move, is to stir up complications and there is no doubt that this ploy succeeds.

18	f5!

Sacrificing a pawn to maintain his light-square grip.

18	...	fxg5
19	hxg5	♖xg5?

The alternative, which may well be better for Black than the text, is 19 ... ♕xg5 20 ♕d5 ♘d8 21 ♖h5 followed by ♖dh1, when White has enormous pressure but Black still has an extra pawn.

20	♕e3	♕f6
21	♘b6 *(51)*	

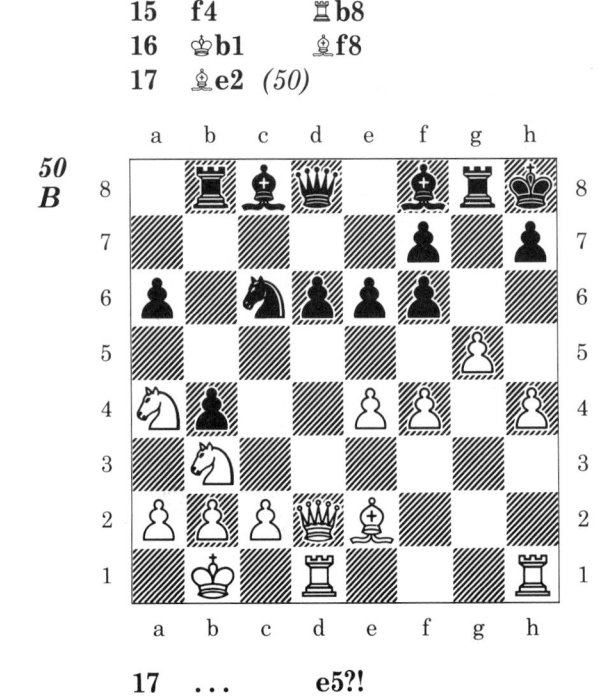

21	...	♘e7
22	♘xc8?	

Plausible enough, but here White overlooks the devastating shot 22 ♗xa6!! ♗xa6 23 ♘d7 when Karpov's position would instantly crumble into ruins. This is further evidence for the view that 19 ... ♕xg5 might have been a superior way of annexing White's pawn.

22	...	♖xc8
23	♗xa6	♖d8
24	♕b6	♘g8
25	♘a5	

Short decides to annihilate what remains of Black's queenside pawns. There was, however, something to be said here for the brutal blockading move 25 ♖d5, simply keeping Black under lock and key.

25	...	d5!

With time trouble looming for both players, Karpov seizes his only chance. After this, the position suddenly gets out of control.

26	♘c6	♖d6
27	exd5	♘e7

28	♕xb4	♘xd5
29	♖xd5?!	*(52)*

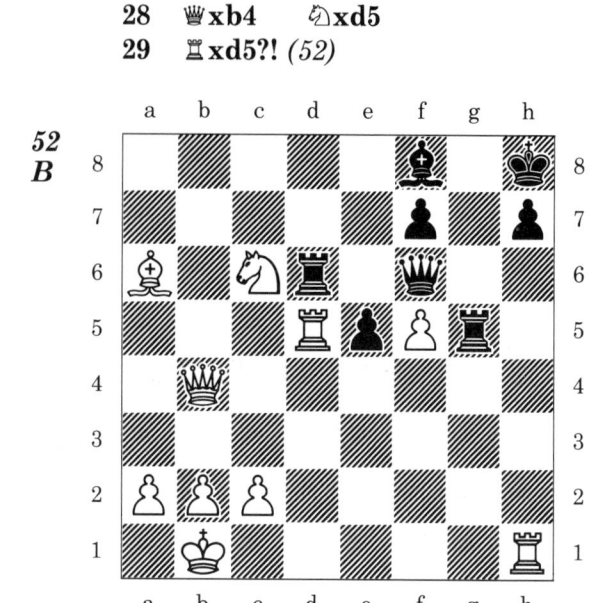

52
B

Apparently murderous, but Black's position is still charged with remarkable resources. 29 ♕h4 would have been safer.

29	...	♕g7?

This amazing move wins White's queen, but Black has to invest too much material for the transaction to be worthwhile. Karpov should have played 29 ... ♖xd5 30 ♕xf8+ ♔g8 31 ♕e7. Now 31 ... ♕xc6 fails to 32 ♕xf7. However, Black can muddy the waters with 31 ... ♕h6!! setting the trap 32 ♖c1 ♕xc1+ 33 ♔xc1 ♖g1+ mating. After 31 ... ♕h6 White could play 32 ♖f1 but once the white rook leaves the h-file, Black can play 32 ... ♕xc6 with impunity leading to a likely win on material.

When quizzed after the game, Nigel claimed that he would have met 31 ... ♕h6 with the astounding 32 a3 ♕xh1+ 33 ♔a2 which he assessed as unclear. White is indeed two exchanges in arrears, but the black king is not at all secure and the white knight threatens to enter play on e5 or e7. Meanwhile, should queens be exchanged, White's armada of queenside pawns is most menacing. Still, Karpov should have

tried this, and it is a great tribute to his fighting spirit that he should have reached a possibility like this after having been reduced to such utter helplessness a mere seven moves beforehand.

30	♖xd6	♖g1+
31	♖d1	♖xd1+
32	♖xd1	♗xb4

White's queen goes but he has too much material.

33	♘xb4	♕g4
34	♖d8+	*(53)*

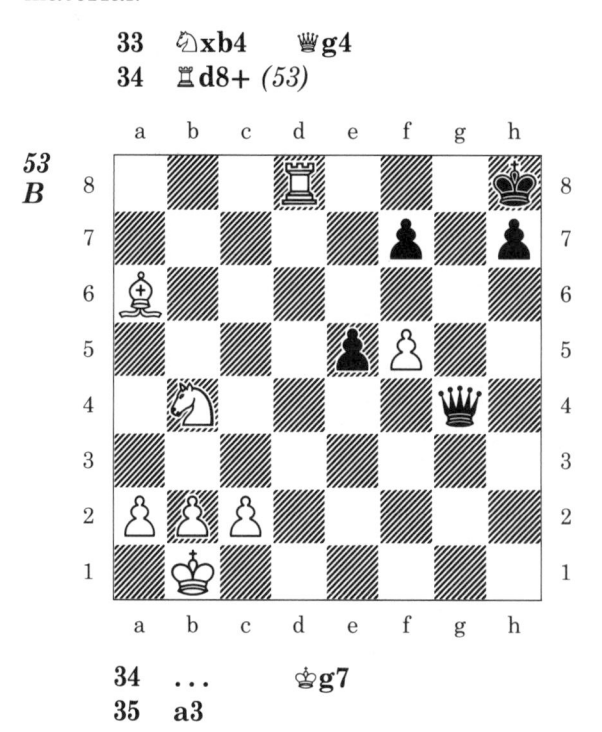

53
B

34	...	♔g7
35	a3	

A neater win is 35 f6+ when 35 ... ♔h6 leaves Black totally tied up while 35 ... ♔g6 permits 37 ♖g8+ skewering the black queen. Finally, 35 ... ♔xf6 36 ♘d5+ ♔g7 (all other moves lose the queen to either a rook or bishop skewer) 37 ♖g8+ ♔xg8 38 ♘f6+ parts Black from his queen in most elegant fashion.

35	...	♕xf5
36	♖d1	h5
37	♖e1	♕e6
38	♗b7	f5
39	♗d5	♕f6
40	c4	e4

41   c5   Black resigns

White's c-pawn will cost Black his queen while the black passed pawns are not much further than the launching pad. Karpov agonised over resigning for half an hour before acquiescing in the inevitable. Living history and high drama combined!

Nigel with Boris Spassky before their encounter at Belfort 1988 (Sabine Kaufman).

GAME ELEVEN

White: Yasser Seirawan
Black: Nigel Short
Amsterdam 1992
Queen's Gambit Declined

The next game in this book shows Nigel wrapping up first place in the Euwe Memorial tournament in Amsterdam, fifteen years after he sensationally beat Penrose. His win here, against a leading American grandmaster, is one of his most complicated ever.

The American Grandmaster Yasser Seirawan (Mark Huba).

1	d4	♘f6
2	c4	e6
3	♘f3	d5

The solid Queen's Gambit, firmly staking a claim in the all-important centre of the board. It is one of Nigel's reliable favourites against 1 d4 and featured heavily in his match against Jan Timman in early 1993.

| 4 | ♘c3 | ♗e7 |
| 5 | ♗f4 | |

5 ♗g5 is the more usual alternative.

5	...	0-0
6	e3	c5
7	dxc5	♗xc5
8	♕c2	♘c6

9 a3 ♛a5 (54)

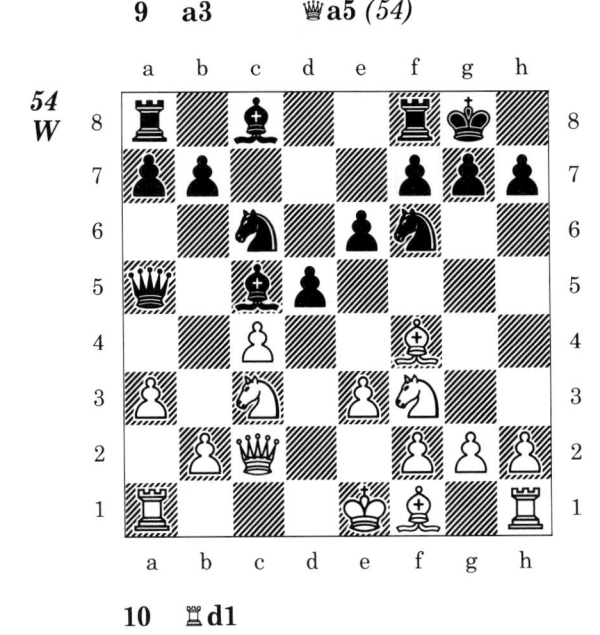

54 W

10 ♖d1

The game which had essentially eliminated Nigel from the previous World Championship cycle was the third game of his 1988 match with Speelman. In that encounter White won brilliantly after 10 0-0-0. Since then, Nigel has devoted enormous effort to preparing against the 5 ♗f4 Queen's Gambit and he was armed to the teeth when he came to this game.

10	...	♗e7
11	♘d2	e5
12	♘b3	♛b6
13	♗g5 (55)	

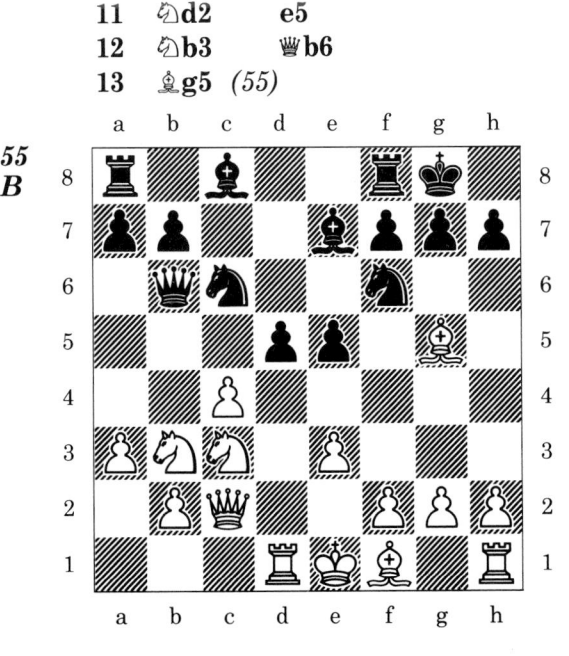

55 B

13 ... ♗e6

An amazing idea which at first sight looks unplayable. It seeks to improve on 13 ... ♗g4 which Nigel had played against Gata Kamsky at Tilburg 1991.

14 ♘a4

Now we see it. The apparently lethal 14 ♗xf6 is met by the intermezzo 14 ... dxc4.

14	...	♛a6
15	cxd5	♛xa4
16	♗xf6	

If 16 dxe6 then 16 ... ♖ac8 leaves White bereft of good moves.

16 ... ♘b4!! (56)

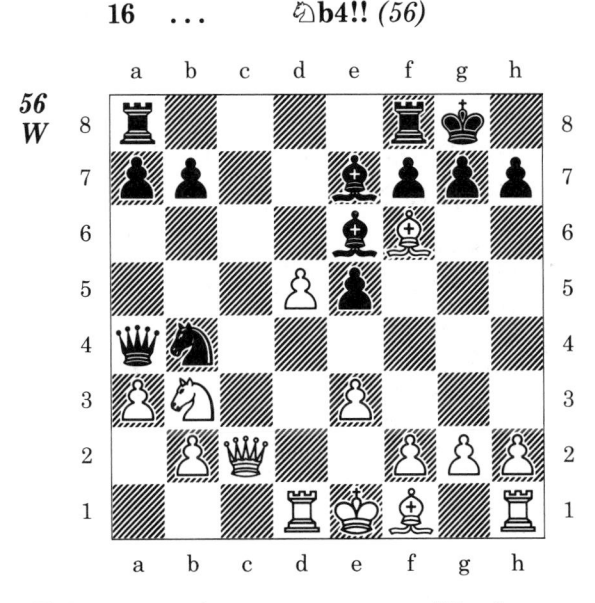

56 W

Without pausing to recapture, Nigel hurls a devastating thunderbolt from an only partially threatening sky. This kind of sudden dynamic resource, combined with his new treatment for White in the Ruy Lopez, makes me feel that Nigel's style is resembling ever more closely that of the great Alekhine. If White accepts the Greek gift with 17 axb4 then 17 ... ♗xb4+ 18 ♔e2 ♖ac8 19 ♛d3 ♗d7 planning ... ♗b5 and ... gxf6, when White is utterly disorganised.

17 ♛e4 ♖ac8

The threat of ... ♘c2+ obliges White to accept the sacrifice.

18 axb4 ♗xb4+
19 ♔e2 (57)

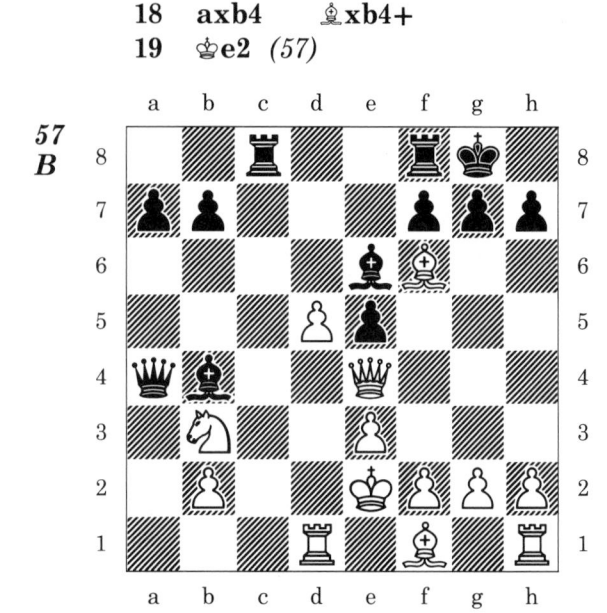

If 19 ♘d2 ♗xd2+ wins White's queen.

19 ... ♕xb3
20 ♗xe5

If 20 dxe6 then 20 ... fxe6 with the horrible threat of ... ♖c2+. This, of course, prevents White's marooned bishop at f6 from escaping.

20 ... ♖c4
21 ♖d4 ♖xd4

22 ♕xd4 ♗xd5 (58)

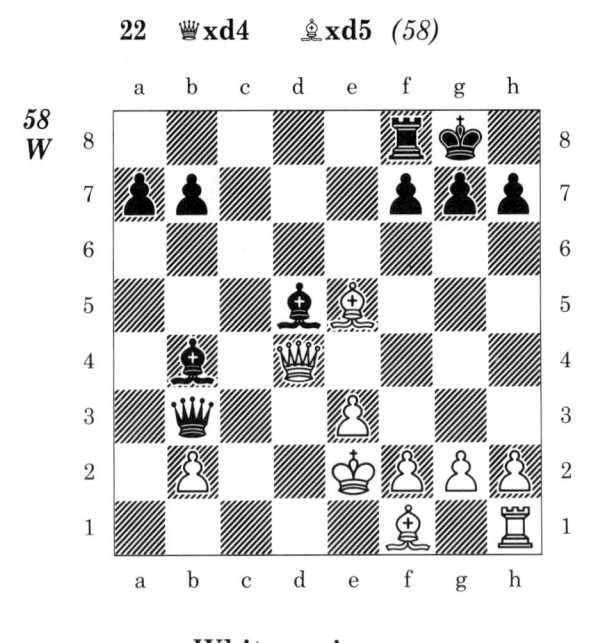

White resigns

White has not even managed to keep any extra material and, with his king and queen his best developed pieces, he has no defence to Black's multiple threats such as ... ♕c2+ or ... ♖d8. It is not often that Black wins so swiftly and dramatically against a leading grandmaster.

58

GAME TWELVE

White: Jan Timman
Black: Nigel Short
World Championship Candidates Final
match (3), El Escorial 1993
Queen's Gambit Declined, Orthodox Variation

At the start of 1993 Nigel Short made chess history when he qualified as the first British grandmaster ever to contest an official World Championship match. Short did this by beating Holland's leading player, Jan Timman in their match at El Escorial, just outside Madrid.

As so often, Nigel kicked off slowly in the match, but he equalised with a brilliant performance in game three, which he later described as his best achievement in the contest. The match was still level-pegging at four points each after eight games, but then Nigel stormed home over the final stretch to win by 7½ to 5½.

Short's opponent in this forthcoming World Championship challenge, Gary Kasparov, personally praised Nigel's superb fighting spirit, which had been the prime factor carrying him through to victory against Timman. Here is that brilliant third game, Nigel's own favourite. I had the pleasure of following this game live, in El Escorial, as it was played. That was certainly an exciting experience, and shows just how wrong those people are who claim that chess does not work as a spectator sport. This game had the audience in the packed Spanish theatre on the edge of their chairs.

1	d4	d5
2	c4	e6
3	♘c3	♘f6

Nigel has discovered that defending the Queen's Gambit with the solid Orthodox Variation is one of the hardest lines for White to crack. Although it has a rather drawish reputation, this is quite wrong, as Nigel has proved against many grandmaster opponents.

4	♗g5	♗e7
5	e3	0-0
6	♘f3	h6

It is important to drive away White's bishop. Sometimes, white players, especially Kasparov himself, resort here to 7 ♗xf6 but Timman prefers to retreat.

7	♗h4	b6

Preparing to place Black's queen's bishop, which is currently shut in, on a promising square on the long light-squared diagonal. Later this bishop creates many dangers for White by constantly threatening to burst into the game.

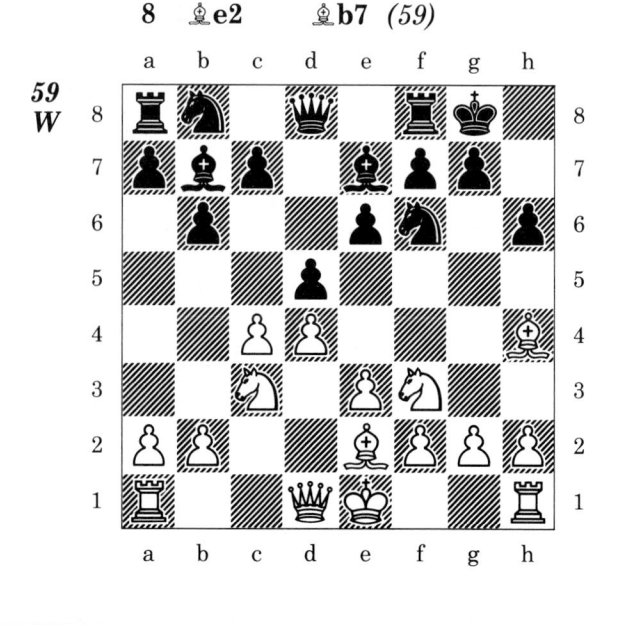

Timman and Short at the 1993 World Championship Candidates Final (Rosa de las Nieves).

8   ♗e2   ♝b7 *(59)*

Only now does Timman decide to trade his bishop for Black's knight, in order to keep Black's queen's bishop locked in behind the pawns.

9	♗xf6	♝xf6
10	cxd5	exd5
11	0-0	♜e8
12	b4	c6

White's plan is to expand on the left flank, hoping to stop Black from playing ... c5 which would free his game.

13	♛b3	a5

60

Alternatives to White's next advance are 14 a3 and 14 bxa5. Both of these had been tried by other grandmasters in the past against Nigel.

14 b5   c5

In the long run it was impossible to hold back this freeing rupture in the centre, so Timman profits from the circumstances to create a passed pawn for himself on the b-file. In an endgame, this could prove a serious danger for Black, so Nigel must try to decide matters before then!

15 dxc5   bxc5
16 ♖ac1   ♗xc3
17 ♕xc3   ♘d7 (60)

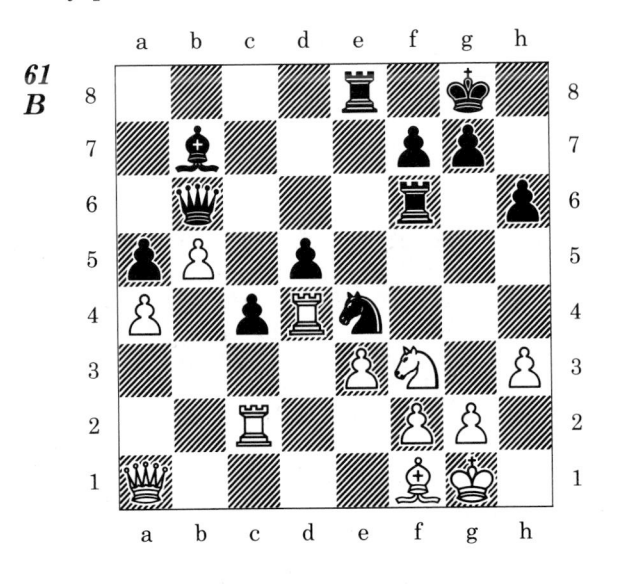

Timman now tries to improve on game one of the same match, in which 18 ♖c2 had been played. White's position looks respectable, but he has no good way of attacking Black's pawns in the centre. In fact, Black's pawns on c5 and d5 actually constitute a flexible weapon, always threatening to advance.

18 ♖fd1   ♕b6
19 ♗f1   ♖ac8
20 h3   ♘f6
21 ♘d2   c4

In the first game ... d4 in similar

circumstances gave Black the initiative. Here, the alternative advance of a black centre pawn turns out to be an extremely fine and dynamic decision. This move is also very risky, in that it gives away occupation of the d4-square to any white piece, and it also makes it much more difficult to resurrect Black's bishop. I can, therefore, well understand why Nigel was so proud of his resolve in making this committal thrust.

22 a4   ♖e6

Planning to mass the artillery of his rooks on the e-file.

23 ♖c2   ♖ce8

Already with the brutal threat ... ♖xe3 which would be a winning sacrifice.

24 ♘f3   ♘e4

The invasion commences.

25 ♕a1   ♖f6
26 ♖d4? (61)

Oblivious to the coming sacrifice. Better is 26 ♘d4, but White's position is already very passive.

26 ...   ♖xf3!!

A superb sacrifice based on the unprotected state of White's rook on c2 and the general undermining of the fortifications around White's king. Timman looked horribly shocked when Nigel played this powerful move.

27 gxf3   ♕g6+

If now 28 ♔h1 ♘g3+ 29 fxg3 ♕xc2, when White's position has more leaks than a rotting hulk.

28 ♗g2   ♘g5

The accumulation of black threats against f3 and c2 mean that Timman must return the material, and more.

| 29 | ♖c1 | ♘xf3+ |
| 30 | ♔f1 | ♘h2+ |

The repetition was just to gain time on the clock, a good practical measure.

31	♔g1	♘f3+
32	♔f1	♘xd4
33	♕xd4	♕f5
34	♔g1	♖e5! *(62)*

A star move. White still has some compensation for his lost pawn in terms of play against Black's pawn on a5 and the temporary inactivity of the black bishop, but this transfer of Black's rook into an attacking posture decides the game.

| 35 | ♕a7 | ♕c8 |
| 36 | ♔f1 | |

With this move and his next, Timman concedes that he has no counterplay left. If 36 ♕xa5 ♖g5 37 f4 ♕xh3 38 fxg5 ♕xe3+ wins easily.

36	...	♖g5
37	♕d4	♕f5
38	f4	♖g6
39	♔f2	♔h7
40	♖d1	♕c2+

This final penetration wins another pawn, while still leaving White's king exposed.

41	♖d2	♕xa4
42	b6	♕b4
43	♖b2	♕e7
44	♖a2	♕h4+ *(63)*

White resigns

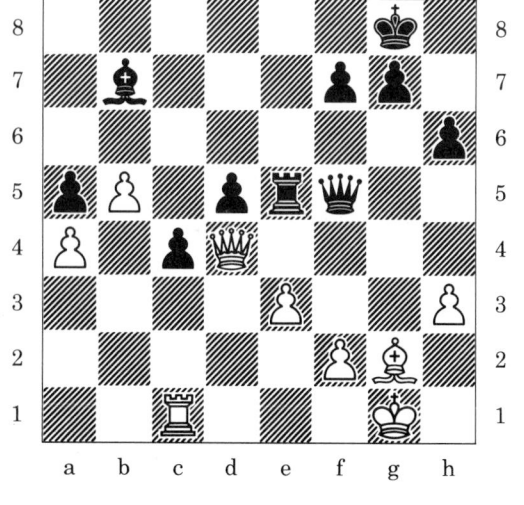

In club play, White might drag it on for a few moves, but Timman was demoralised and recognised that Nigel would easily win with his extra pawns and the attack.

A fitting game with which to end this book, and look forward to his historic challenge against Kasparov.

The next World Champion?